iLLUSTRATiON
BOOK PRO 02

イラストレーション ブック プロ 02

Edited by pict

アーティストエージェンシー・ピクト編

Foreword:

Adrian Shaughnessy

Editor in Chief of "Varoom" magazine

Profile

Adrian Shaughnessy is a designer, art director and writer. He co-founded the London design studio Intro, leaving in 2004 to pursue an interest in writing, and to work as an independent design consultant. Today he runs ShaughnessyWorks, a design and editorial consultancy. He has written and art directed numerous books on design including "How to be a Graphic Designer Without Losing Your Soul."

Shaughnessy is editor of "Varoom": the journal of illustration and made images, and writes regularly for leading design publications and blogs. He hosts a radio show called Graphic Design on the Radio, on Resonance FM.

Varoom 07
Editor : Adrian Shaughnessy
Design : Non-Format
Illustration : Jasper Goodall
Varoom is published by the AOI
www.varoom-mag.com

Illustration is everywhere. We wear it on t-shirts; advertisers use it to sell everything from MP3 players to fashion accessories; graphic novels compete with traditional novels; comic books get made into Hollywood movies; Manga is a growing obsession in the West; and Banksy has become an international art world sensation selling his work in galleries in LA, London and Tokyo. We even buy books full of illustration – welcome to "Illustration Book Pro 02"

Today, illustration has gone supernova. Degree courses in universities around the world are full of ambitious illustration students; new talent is bursting out of Brazil, China, Mexico and a dozen other countries around the world; when brands want to speak to young hip audiences, illustration is increasingly the preferred way to do it. It's a global lingua franca of image and colour. As a look through the pages of this book will confirm, illustration comes in a myriad of shapes and forms. Illustration is now so diverse that no one is quite sure what the craft is anymore. For the past few decades, illustration has been eclipsed by photography as the form of visual expression most likely to attract the attention of media savvy consumers: this is no longer the case, and illustration is moving back to centre stage, a position it last held in the 1970s. Also, a growing number of illustrators are selling prints to the public rather than waiting for their next commercial commission. And a new breed of illustration collectives is replacing the solitary individual working alone in a studio. These are big changes in the illustration landscape: illustration is no longer the sleepy backwater of visual communication that it has been in recent decades.

Amongst all this ebb and flux, one thing is certain – illustrators can no longer afford to be passive. Opportunities may be plentiful, but making a living as an illustrator is not easy. Most illustration assignments are poorly paid in comparison to the fees earned by graphic designers and photographers; only advertising agencies can afford to pay top rates. But, illustrators are resourceful, and a more entrepreneurial generation has emerged that is vigorously exploring fresh ways of working and different ways of generating income.

This new breed is active: it holds exhibitions, starts fashion labels, produces street art, self-publishes books and magazines, and sells original prints in galleries and online. Inexpensive digital printing means that illustrators can now sell their work cheaply and easily to a growing army of illustration fans. A host of websites has sprung up offering high quality signed prints by leading illustrators to an eager public.

This rise in self-initiated work is hardly surprising. Unlike other forms of commercial visual communication such as graphic design, branding, and TV commercials, where practitioners usually have to submerge there own personal voices, illustrators are encouraged to retain their personal signatures. This is one of the things that makes illustration so attractive: we recognise the styles of favourite illustrators – their identities shine through in their work.

But while more and more people are drawn to illustration, and while the standard seems stunningly high, it is also true to say that much of the work that we see is hard to place geographically, and seems to have shed its national characteristics. It's good to know that illustrators based in Rio can work for clients based in London; its good to know that Japanese illustrators can work for French brand owners. But does the globalisation of visual culture lead to a featureless uniformity? Is there a British style? An American style? A Japanese style?

Looking at the work in this book, I'm bound to say that much of it looks as if it could have been created anywhere in the world. This is hardly surprising; the internet, increased foreign travel, and newly globalized media networks – not to mention the near-universal use of the computer – are all bound to have a homogenising effect on illustrators around the world. It is unavoidable. And yet within these pages, a Japanese accent still remains. We can clearly see that many of the illustrations have a link with the glorious heritage of Japanese woodblocks, with the art of ukiyo-e ("pictures of the floating world"), and with the noble tradition of Japanese calligraphy and penmanship.

Personally, I'll be disappointed if national characteristics are totally eradicated from illustration. But my prediction is that, as always happens in art and design, some creative force will emerge which will make us all revisit our national heritages.

エイドリアン・ショーネシー

『Varoom』編集長

プロフィール

デザイナー、アートディレクター、ライター。ロンドンのデザインスタジオ、Introの共同設立者。執筆活動、デザインコンサルタントのキャリアを追求するため2004年にスタジオから独立し、目下、デザインと編集のコンサルティングShaughnessyWorksを運営。『How to be a Graphic Designer Without Losing Your Soul（日本語版「魂を失わずにグラフィックデザイナーになる本」ピエ・ブックス刊）』など、多くのデザイン関連書籍の執筆やアートディレクションに携わる。また彼はイラストレーションと創作イメージの雑誌『Varoom』の編集長でもあり、他にも定期的に主要デザイン雑誌やブログに執筆している。ロンドンのFM局Resonance FMでは、Graphic Design on the Radioという番組も担当している。

Varoom 07
編集：エイドリアン・ショーネシー
デザイン：Non-Format
イラストレーション：ジャスパー・グッドール
出版：the AOI
www.varoom-mag.com

　イラストレーションは世界中にあふれかえっている。私たちが普段愛用するTシャツにも、MP3プレイヤーからアクセサリーまでさまざまな商品の広告にも。そしてグラフィックノベルは普通の小説と肩を並べ、ハリウッドはこぞってコミックブックを映画化しようとする。日本のマンガの西洋での人気は高まるばかりだし、覆面アーティストのバンクシーはいまや美術界の寵児となり、その作品はロサンゼルスやロンドン、東京のギャラリーで売買されている。何より、イラストレーションしか載っていない本書のような本を買う人たちさえいるのだ ── そう、『イラストレーションブックプロ02』の世界にようこそ。

　今日、イラストレーションは隆盛を極めている。美術大学は、どこにいってもイラストレーター志望の学生たちでいっぱいだ。ブラジルや中国、メキシコほか世界中のあらゆる場所から次々と新たな才能が飛び出してくる。企業にしても、ヒップな若者層をターゲットにするときは、イラストレーションを使って訴えようとするケースが増えている。イラストレーションは、イメージとカラーからなる世界共通言語だからだ。

　本書を見てもらえばわかるとおり、一口にイラストレーションといっても、そのかたちは実にさまざまだ。むしろ多様すぎて、もはや何をもってイラストレーションと呼ぶのか分からないぐらいだ。ここ数十年ほど、メディアにおける主役は写真だった。イラストレーションよりも写真のほうが、流行に敏感な人々の注目を集めやすい表現だと考えられていた。だが、それも過去の話である。イラストレーションが、1970年代以来久しぶりにまたステージの中央に

戻ってきたのだ。それと同時に、多くのイラストレーターが、企業からの依頼を待つ代わりに、自分の作品を一般に直接販売するようにもなった。また、イラストレーターの台頭は、アトリエでひとり孤独に制作に励むアーティストのイメージを過去のものにした。イラストレーションを取り巻く環境は大きく変化した。イラストレーションはもう、しばらくずっとそう考えられていたような、時代に取り残されたビジュアル表現ではなくなったのだ。

　こうした時代の趨勢のなかで、ひとつ確実なことがある。もはやイラストレーターは、受け身ではいられないということだ。チャンスが増えたとはいえ、イラストレーターとして食べていくのは容易なことではない。イラストレーターの仕事に対する報酬が、グラフィックデザイナーや写真家に比べて低いのは事実だ。しかも、高報酬を約束できるのは大手広告代理店に限られる。だがイラストレーターという人々は、機智に富んだ人種でもある。とりわけ起業家精神にあふれた新世代は、新しい仕事の形や収入を生むためのさまざまな方法を積極的に探し求めるようになった。

　彼ら新世代は実に意欲的だ。展覧会を企画したり、ファッションブランドを立ち上げたり、ストリートアートに挑戦したり、作品集や雑誌を自費出版したり、オリジナルプリントをギャラリーやオンラインで販売したりする。コストの低いデジタル印刷の登場とともに、今日のイラストレーターは、自分の作品を気軽に安く、増え続けるイラストレーションファンに売ることが可能なのだ。実際、インターネット上では、いくつものウェブサイトが誕生し、一流イラストレーターの署名入り高画質プリントを、それらを熱心に求める人々へ販売している。

　イラストレーターによるこうした自発的な動きは、ある意味当然のことだったかもしれない。商業的なビジュアル表現の世界では、たとえばグラフィックデザインやブランディング、あるいはテレビCMなどの場合、それに関わるクリエイター個人の視点を大々的に表面に出すことはできない。ところがイラストレーターは、むしろ独自のスタイルを際立たせることを求められている。だからこそ、イラストレーションは魅力的なのだ。私たちは、商業ビジュアルのなかにも、お気に入りのイラストレーターのスタイルを見つけることができる。彼らのアイデンティティは、その作品から透けて見えてくる。

　だが、イラストレーションの魅力に開眼する人が増え、作品のクオリティもかつてないほど高くなっている一方で、世界的に作品が均質化し、その国ならではの個性が失われているのもまた事実である。もちろん、リオデジャネイロ在住のイラストレーターが、ロンドンのクライアントのために仕事をしたり、日本人イラストレーターがフランスのファッションブランドの仕事を請け負えるようになったのは素晴らしいことだ。しかしビジュアル文化のグローバル化は、そのまま特徴のない画一性に結びついてしまうのだろうか？　いま、英国スタイルというものは存在するだろうか？　アメリカンスタイルは？　そして日本スタイルは？

　本書に収められた作品を見るかぎり、そのほとんどは、世界のどの場所で生み出されていてもおかしくないと言わざるをえない。それも不思議なことではない。インターネット、気軽になった海外旅行、グローバル化されたメディアネットワークの誕生、そして一家に一台の勢いで普及するコンピューター。そうしたすべての要素が、世界中のイラストレーターの均質化をもたらす。それはもう避けられないことだ。それでもやはり、私は本書のそこここに日本らしさを見い出す。いくつかの作品は、明らかに浮世絵という日本の輝かしい遺産とのつながりを感じさせてくれる。また別の作品には、高貴な伝統である書道の痕跡が見受けられる。

　個人的には、イラストレーションから完全にその国らしさが失われてしまうところは見たくない。だがきっと、アートやデザインが常にそうであるように、必ずまた何かしらの「創造的な力」が現れて、私たちを再び自分の国の遺産に向き合わせてくれることだろう。

Latest projects of PICT PICTの仕事実績

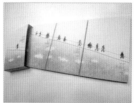

01 Starbucks Coffee Japan, Ltd. / プロモーションビジュアル　奈路道程
02 CONVERSE / SPORTSWEAR INTERNATIONAL YEAR BOOK　KO-ZOU
03 ELLE DECORATION (UK) / 永宮陽子
04 COSMOS BOOKS (HK) / ブックカバー　みずうちさとみ
05 ESPRIT / SPORTSWEAR INTERNATIONAL YEAR BOOK　KO-ZOU
06 SPEEDSTAR RECORDS / 08'レミオロメンツアーパンフレット　柴田ケイコ

07 アルビオン化粧品 / 「EPRISE Sound&Picnic」　東ちなつ
08 キヤノン (HK) / Canon EXPO 2007　イマイヤスフミ
09 JOHN RICHMOND / SPORTSWEAR INTERNATIONAL YEAR BOOK　Licaco
10 A.F. VANDEVORST / SPORTSWEAR INTERNATIONAL YEAR BOOK　宮島亜希

Contact : info@pict-web.com
お仕事に関するお問い合わせ、ご依頼につきましては317ページのPICTのシステムをご覧ください。

01 エイチビー・ジャパン株式会社 / Harper's BAZAAR　Licaco
02 株式会社Hit&Run / ワカ天 Hit&Runちゃん祭り2007　マグマジャイアンツ
03 ヒルトンプラザ ウエスト / 電照コルトン柱　長谷川ひとみ
04 エイベックス / Koda Kumi LiveTour 08 パンフレット　micca
05 LTB Jeans / SPORTSWEAR INTERNATIONAL YEAR BOOK　micca
06 アルク / 冊子表紙　中川学

07 PUMA / SPORTSWEAR INTERNATIONAL YEAR BOOK　サイトウユウスケ
08 株式会社 毎日コミュニケーションズ / エスカーラ・リン　長谷川洋子
09 マガジンハウス / Hanako　さとうあゆみ
10 バカルディジャパン株式会社 / Bombay Sapphire Botanical Art Glass /
　　Artists：小野亮　木村敏子　ショウヘイタカサキ　田名部敏文　廣田明香　Photographer：望月 孝
11 iSKO / SPORTSWEAR INTERNATIONAL YEAR BOOK　内田文武

Latest projects of PICT PICTの仕事実績

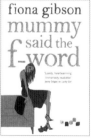

01	02	03
04		05
06	07	08
09	10	11

01 TIME ZONE / SPORTSWEAR INTERNATIONAL YEAR BOOK　MACHIKO
02 講談社 / 「偽装建築国家」書籍カバー　安瀬英雄
03 ミューザ川崎シンフォニーホール / フェスタサマーミューザヴィジュアル　山口絵美
04 PePe Jeans / SPORTSWEAR INTERNATIONAL YEAR BOOK　サイトウユウスケ
05 Orange / WAD magazine　加藤彩
06 ベネッセコーポレーション / 作文チャレンジ　イマイヤスフミ

07 東急百貨店 / クリスマスビジュアル　tupera tupera
08 OSKLEN / SPORTSWEAR INTERNATIONAL YEAR BOOK　宮島亜希
09 GQ(France)　ミヤタジロウ
10 HODDER & SROUGHTON / 書籍カバー　さとうあゆみ
11 竜の子プロダクション / MACH 5 LINE PROJECT　福田透
©2008 Tatsunoko Production designed by TORU FUKUDA

Contact : info@pict-web.com
お仕事に関するお問い合わせ、ご依頼につきましては317ページのPICTのシステムをご覧ください。

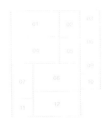

01 JORDACHE/SPORTSWEAR INTERNATIONAL YEAR BOOK　Licaco
02 「恋するマドリ」MOVIE+DVD　河村ふうこ
03 清水菓舗「かさね三盆」/ Webサイト　松尾ミユキ
04 BOSSA/SPORTSWEAR INTERNATIONAL YEAR BOOK　MACHIKO
05 株式会社ぱど / L'ala Pado　吉濱あさこ
06 三省堂 / クラウン総合英語　デザイン/天野誠（magic beans）　平田利之

07 ISSEY MIYAKE INC./ ELTTOB TEP ISSEY MIYAKE "THE BOTTLE MAIL"　宮島亜希
08 The creator studio /　宮島亜希
09 LE BOOK /パッケージ　内田文武
10 日本コカ・コーラ / Minute Park　仲里カズヒロ
11 オフィス・シロウズ / office shirousウェブサイト　ヒラノトシユキ
12 BETSEY JOHNSON/SPORTSWEAR INTERNATIONAL YEAR BOOK　加藤大

Editorial note エディトリアルノート

Credit format クレジットフォーマット

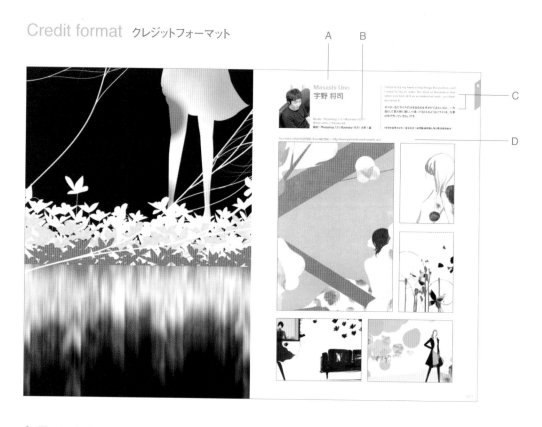

A Illustrator's name イラストレーター名

B Media 画材

C Is there any project you would like to do in the future ? 今後手がけたい仕事

D Web site address ウェブサイトアドレス

iLLUSTRATiON BOOK PRO 02

イラストレーション ブック プロ 02

さらに進化を続けるジャパンイラストレーション
次なるトレンドがここに集結

Edited by pict

アーティストエージェンシー・ピクト編

Hana Akiyama
秋山 花

Media : Acrylic / Pencil / Drawing paper /
Illustration board
画材：アクリル / 鉛筆 / 画用紙 / イラストボード

Book design, CD cover illustration, magazine illustration, t-shirt design, picture books. I want to do illustration work in a variety of fields, fashion, interior, advertising, and books. I also want to actively participate in work in other countries.

本の装丁、CDカバーイラスト、雑誌イラスト、Tシャツイラスト、絵本。ファッション、インテリア、広告、書籍、様々な分野でイラストをとおして仕事をしていきたい。海外での仕事も積極的に参加していきたい。

1984年東京生まれ / 東京在住 / 多摩美術大学大学院美術研究科修了

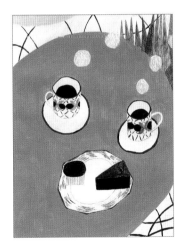

Kenji Asazuma
浅妻 健司

Media : Acrylic
画材：アクリル絵の具

I want to expand into advertising and cover art work.

広告や装画の仕事を広げていきたい。

1974年横浜生まれ / 横浜在住 / セツ・モードセミナー卒

あ

See more artwork（バリエーションはこちら）>> http://www.pict-web.com/kenji_asazuma

Hiroshi Asami
浅見 広志

Media : Cray / Acrylic / Digital camera /
Photo matt paper / Pastel
画材：石粉粘土 / アクリル絵具 /
デジタル一眼レフカメラ / フォトマット紙 / パステル

I want to be widely active in things like advertising, CD jackets, or magazines. I'm also interested in expressions in which I can transmit my interpretation of the world, like producing action figures.

雑誌、CDジャケット、広告など幅広く活動したいです。クリエイターフィギュアの制作など自分から世界観を発進していく表現にも興味があります。

1978年千葉県生まれ / 埼玉在住
東洋美術学校グラフィックデザイン科卒

Azumimushi
あずみ虫

Media : Acrylic gouache / Aluminium
画材：アクリルガッシュ / アルミ板

1975年神奈川生まれ / 東京在住 / コム・イラストレーターズ・スタジオ卒

I'm interested in advertising work that is cool without any reason. And, I'd also like to try to draw picture books which I like since long time ago.

理屈抜きにかっこ良い、広告の仕事に興味があります。又、昔から好きな絵本も描いてみたいです。

See more artwork（バリエーションはこちら）>> http://www.pict-web.com/azumimushi

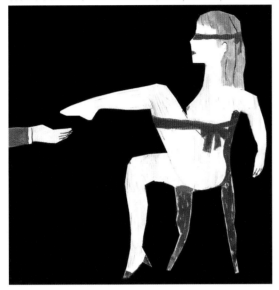

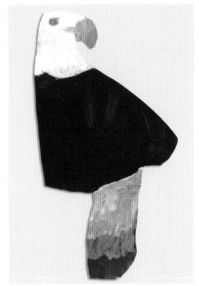

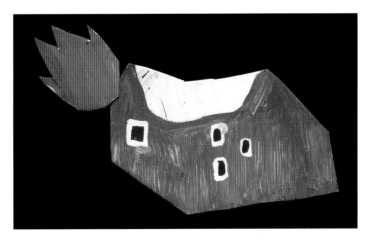

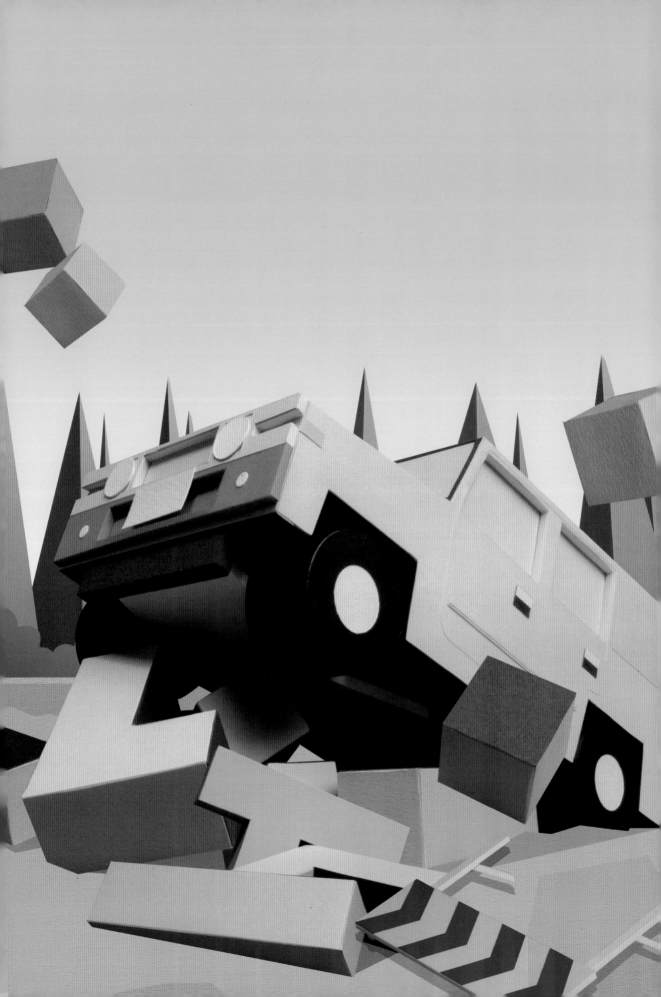

Hideo Anze
安瀬 英雄

Media : Styrene board / Paper / Digital camera /
Photoshop CS
画材 : スチレンボード / 紙 / デジタルカメラ /
Photoshop CS

My ideal work is mainly advertising, book design,
magazines, etc. However, I think it would be great
if I could try my hand at more of the kind of things
people can actually touch and are a part of their
daily lives, like book design and magazines.

主に広告、装丁、雑誌などの仕事が理想ですが、装丁や雑誌
など実際に人の手に触れ生活の一部にあるようなものをより
多く手がけられたらと思います。

1975年東京都生まれ / 神奈川在住 / 武蔵野美術大学短期大学部中退

See more artwork（バリエーションはこちら）>> http://www.pict-web.com/hideo_anze

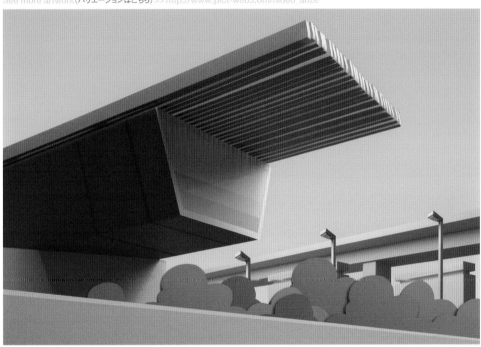

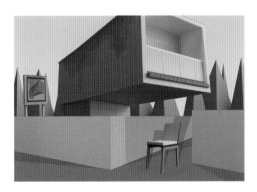

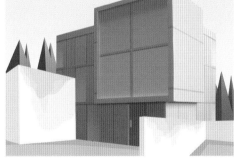

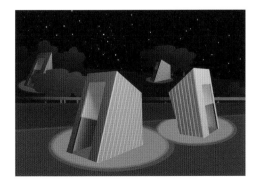

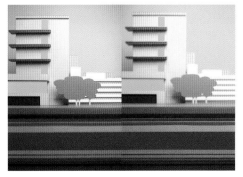

Kosuke Ikeda
池田 孝友

Media : Gel ink ballpoint pen /
Mechanical pencil / Paper
画材：ゲルインクボールペン / シャーペン / 紙

Cover art and design for books, magazines, etc.,
movie posters, product labels, TV commercials,
posters for tourist areas where things like old town
streets remain, kimono design, etc.

本、雑誌などの装丁画、映画ポスター、商品のラベル、テレビ
CM、古い町並みなどが残る観光地のポスター、着物の模様
など。

1979年大阪府生まれ / 京都在住 / 独学

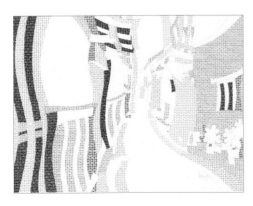

Sachiko Ikoma
生駒 さちこ

Media : Water color
画材：水彩

I'm interested in book design, fashion illustrations, product development, textiles, travel diaries, food, etc. Basically, because I want to do anything, I'm not limited by the media. First, I want to do a bunch of different things.

本の装丁、ファッションイラスト、グッズ展開、テキスタイル、旅日記、食などに興味あり。基本、なんでもやりたいほうなので、メディアを限定するつもりはありません。まずはいろいろなことをやってみたい。

1971年京都生まれ / 東京在住 / セツ・モードセミナー卒

See more artwork（バリエーションはこちら）>> http://www.pict-web.com/sachiko_ikoma

Rika Ishii
石井 利佳

I think that I'd like to do work that remains in someone's heart, regardless of the media.

媒体にかかわらず、誰かの心に残る仕事をしていけたらと思います。

Media : Photoshop CS
画材 : Photoshop CS

1978年東京生まれ / 静岡在住

Shizuka Ishizaka
石坂 しづか

Media : Photoshop CS2 / Color pencil / Pencil
画材 : Photoshop CS2 / 色鉛筆 / 鉛筆

I want to try my hand at moving pictures like animation. I've tried my hand at textile design, and it's charming work, so if I have the opportunity, I think I want to try to work it again.

アニメーションなど、動画を手がけてみたいと思っています。テキスタイルデザインは手がけたことがありますが、魅力的な仕事なので、機会があったらまた制作してみたいと思っています。

1971年東京生まれ / 東京在住 / 桑沢デザイン研究所卒

See more artwork (バリエーションはこちら) >> http://www.pict-web.com/shizuka_ishizaka

Hiroki Itagaki
板垣 広樹

General visual images in music, fashion, books, etc.

音楽、服飾、書籍などのビジュアルイメージ全般。

Media : Illustrator CS / Photoshop CS
画材 : Illustrator CS / Photoshop CS

1974年埼玉県生まれ / 東京都在住

See more artwork(バリエーションはこちら) >> http://www.pict-web.com/hiroki_itagaki

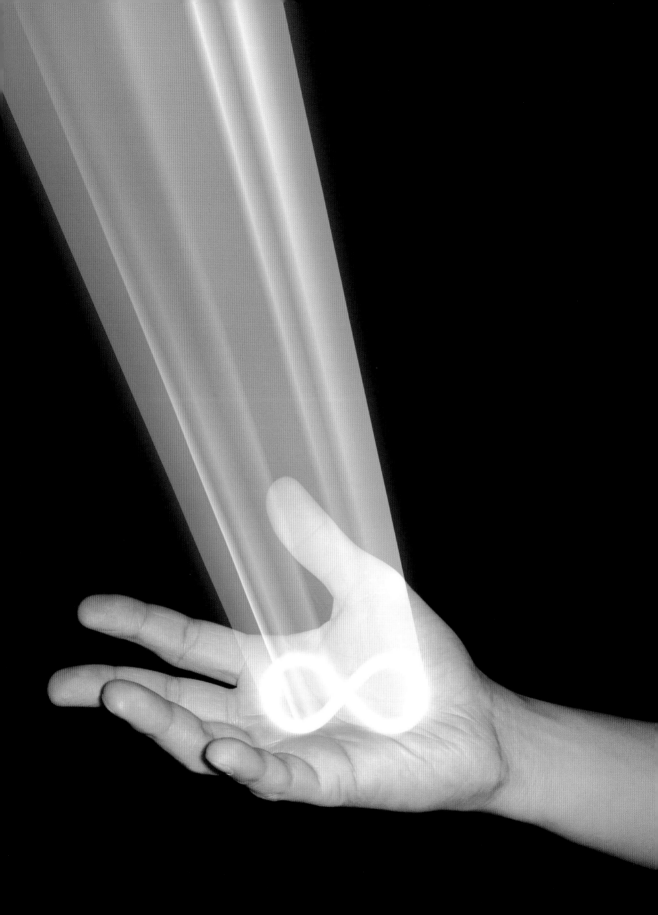

IPPI
IPPI 松谷 一飛

Media : Photoshop CS3 / Illustrator CS3 / Cyber-shot

画材 : Photoshop CS3 / Illustrator CS3 / Cyber-shot
Every creation. Expressing something new. Then I hope it will become a good creation.

あらゆる制作。新しい何かを表現すること。そしてそれが良いクリエイションになることを願っています。

京都生まれ / 東京在住

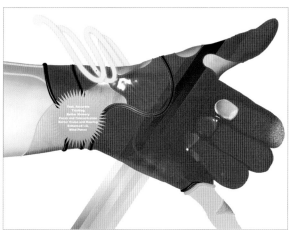

YUJIN ITO
伊藤 友人

I would like to try to do things like illustrations that engage with magazine covers, book covers, CD jackets, and television programs.

雑誌の表紙、書籍装画、CDジャケット、テレビ番組と連動したイラストなどをやってみたいです。

Media : Acrylic gouache / Medium / Drawing paper
画材：アクリルガッシュ / メディウム / 画用紙

1970年東京都生まれ / 東京在住 / セツ・モードセミナー卒

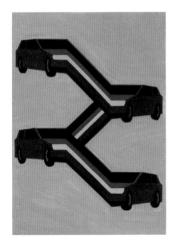

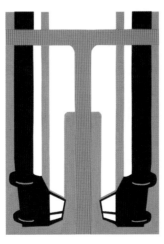

Akari Inoguchi
猪口 燈

Media : Photoshop CS2 / Acrylic / Pencil / Color pencil
画材：Photoshop CS2 / アクリル絵の具 / 鉛筆 / 色鉛筆

In the future, I would like to become more involved in traditional Japanese crafts, such as decorative mural painting and designing textile patterns for kimonos. Living abroad, for over a decade now, I have developed a renewed appreciation for the beauty of traditional Japanese art.

海外に長く住むことによって、日本の良い所を改めて、見直す様になりました。日本の伝統芸術である、室内壁画や、着物の柄のデザインなどに関わった仕事をしてみたいです。

1974年生まれ / NY在住 / Fine Arts, Hunter College

Yasufumi Imai
イマイ ヤスフミ

Media : Illustrator CS
画材 : Illustrator CS

1972年大阪府生まれ / 大阪在住 /
大阪芸術大学グラフィックデザイン科卒

I want to move to try my hand at work with goods
and products for campaigns, also 3D or animation.

キャンペーンなどのグッズや商品、また3Dやアニメーションの
仕事なども手がけていきたいです。

See more artwork（バリエーションはこちら）>> http://www.pict-web.com/yasufumi_imai

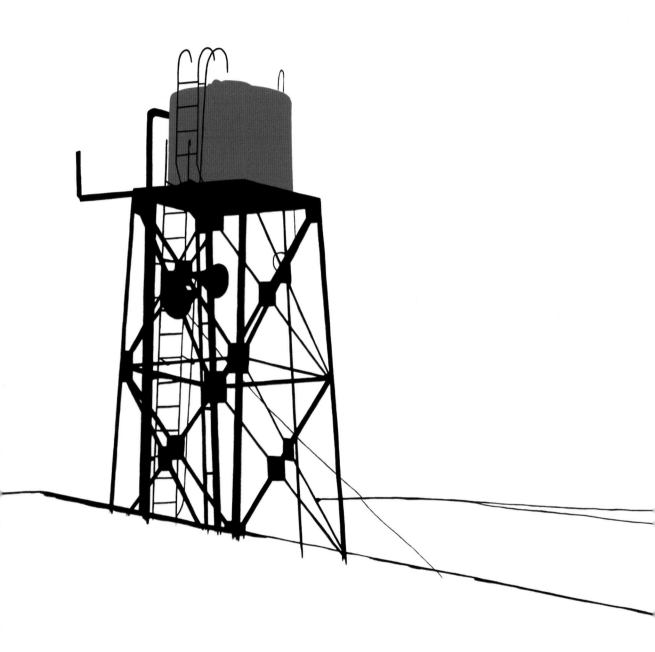

Fumitake Uchida
内田 文武

Media : Photoshop CS / Acrylic / Pencil
画材：Photoshop CS / アクリル / 鉛筆

Cover art for novels, and public art. I think that I want to make the kind of things that go beyond genres or disciplines, and are not consumed by the people who see them.

小説の装画やパブリックアート、分野や媒体を越えて一人の人にとっては消費ではなくそこから生まれるようなモノを作りたいと思います。

1981年京都府生まれ / 京都在住 / 京都造形芸術大学美術工芸学科卒

See more artwork（バリエーションはこちら）>> http://www.pict-web.com/fumitake_uchida

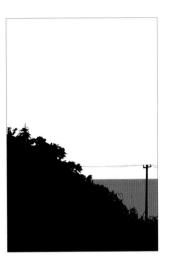

"Welcome to the world of Le book"

Masashi Uno
宇野 将司

Media : Photoshop 7.0 / Illustrator 10.0 /
Water color / Chinese ink
画材 : Photoshop 7.0 / Illustrator 10.0 / 水彩 / 墨

I want to try my hand at big things like posters, and I want to try to make the kind of illustration that when you look at it as an individual work, you think you want it.

ポスターなどサイズの大きなものを手がけてみたいのと、一作品として見た時に欲しいと思ってもらえるようなイラストを、仕事の中で作っていきたいです。

1978年岐阜生まれ / 東京在住 / 岐阜聖徳学園大学付属高等学校卒

See more artwork (バリエーションはこちら) >> http://www.pict-web.com/masashi_uno

Tadashi Ura
ウラタダシ

Media : Photoshop CS / Illustrator CS /
Chinese ink / Water color / Pencil / Pen /
Japanese paper
画材 : Photoshop CS / Illustrator CS / 墨 / 水彩 /
鉛筆 / ペン / 和紙

I want to make pictures that capture the inspiration
that one feels in stories, like novel cover design /
art, picture book creation, etc. Also things that
introduce facilities and places in which history and
traditions remain, like websites, concept books etc.

小説の装丁画や絵本制作など、物語に感じるインスピレーシ
ョンを絵にしたい。また歴史や伝統が残る場所・施設の紹介
サイトやコンセプトブックなど。

1972年長崎県生まれ / 東京在住 / 日本デザイナー学院グラフィックデザイン科卒

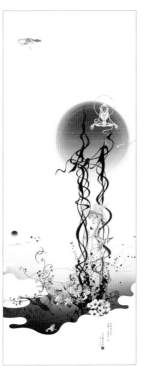

Naoya Enomoto
榎本 直哉

Media : Illustrator CS / Photoshop CS / Pencil /
Water color / Collage
画材 : Illustrator CS / Photoshop CS / 鉛筆 / 水彩 /
コラージュ

Illustrations used in magazines, published in
places like graphic's journals, visual images in
advertising, book design, textiles, graphics on
packaging, etc.

雑誌で使用するイラスト、グラフィック誌などへの掲載、広告で
のビジュアルイメージ、装丁、テキスタイル、パッケージのグラフ
ィックなど。

1980年神奈川県生まれ / 神奈川在住 / 東京工芸大学デザイン学科卒

Aya Ota
太田 彩

Media : Color pen / Ink / Pencil
画材：カラーペン / インク / 鉛筆

It is a great pleasure to be able to encounter new discoveries and inspiration while drawing. I think I'd like to be widely active, regardless of the genre.

お仕事をすることで、描いている際に新しい発見や刺激に出会えることは楽しみのひとつです。ジャンルにかかわらず、幅広く活動していきたいと思っています。

1975年愛媛県生まれ / 東京在住 /
東京ファッションアカデミーファッションデザイン科卒

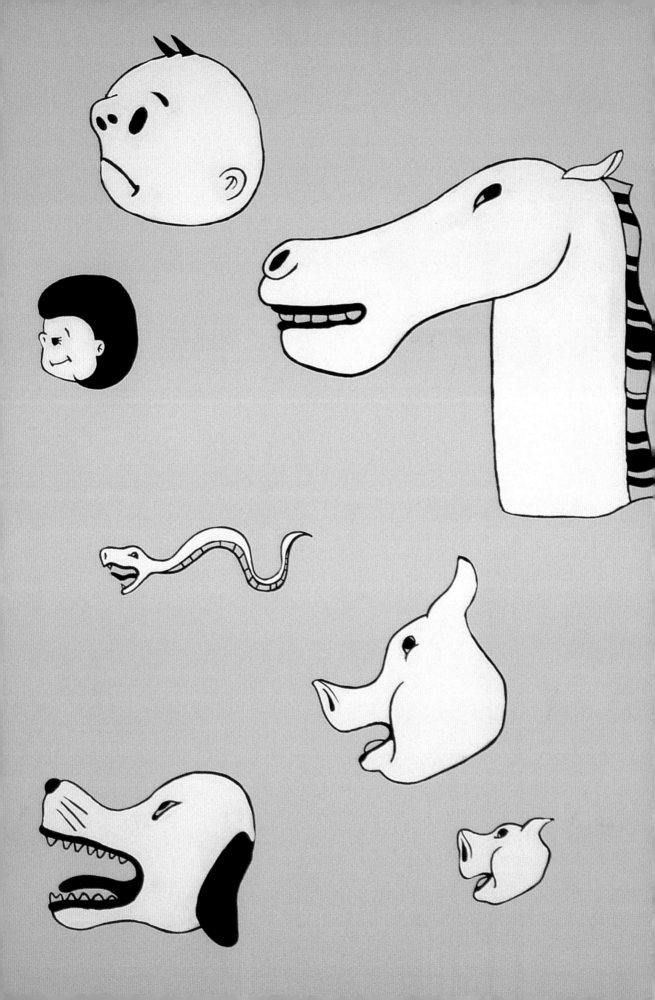

大西 洋

Media : Acrylic
画材：アクリル

I've had lots of work in advertising, but I'd like to get involved in various media like fashion, animation, etc., with pictures and works related to music.

広告でのお仕事が多いのですが、音楽と関わりのある仕事や絵を素材として、ファッションやアニメーションなど様々な媒体にも関わっていきたい。

1976年東京生まれ / 東京在住 / 東京藝術大学デザイン科卒

Ayame Ono
大野 彩芽

Media : Photoshop 7.0 / Illustrator 10 / Paste / Scissors / Pencil
画材 : Photoshop 7.0 / Illustrator 10 / 糊 / はさみ / 鉛筆

I'm interested in printing since I've worked on books, and I'm also interested in advertising, fashion, and artwork related to music.

本というかたちでずっと作品を作ってきたので、書籍や、また、広告・ファッション・音楽関係のアートワークなどにも興味があります。

1982年東京生まれ / 東京在住 /
多摩美術大学大学院美術研究科デザイン専攻卒

053

MIYUKI OHASHI
大橋 美由紀

Media : Acrylic / Crayon / Pencil
画材：アクリル / クレヨン / 鉛筆

Collection reports, working in brand fashion. Work related to ladies', men's, and children's fashion.

コレクションリポートやファッションブランドとのコラボレーション。レディース、メンズ、キッズファッション関連の仕事。

1976年栃木県生まれ / 埼玉在住 / セツ・モードセミナー卒

See more artwork（バリエーションはこちら）>> http://www.pict-web.com/miyuki_ohashi

TOKO OHMORI

大森 とこ

Media : Photoshop 7.0 / Water color / Acrylic / Pencil / Photo / Newspaper

画材 : Photoshop 7.0 / 水彩 / アクリル / 鉛筆 / 写真 / 新聞

Things that are used in daily life like textiles or goods, or things that you can print (visuals), things that broaden the world perspective of the people and things I draw.

テキスタイル、グッズなど生活用品のものやヴィジュアルを印刷できるもの、自分の描く人や物の世界観が広がっていけるもの。

1971年山口県生まれ / 東京都在住 / 東京造形大学美術一類学科卒

See more artwork（バリエーションはこちら）>> http://www.pict-web.com/toko_ohmori

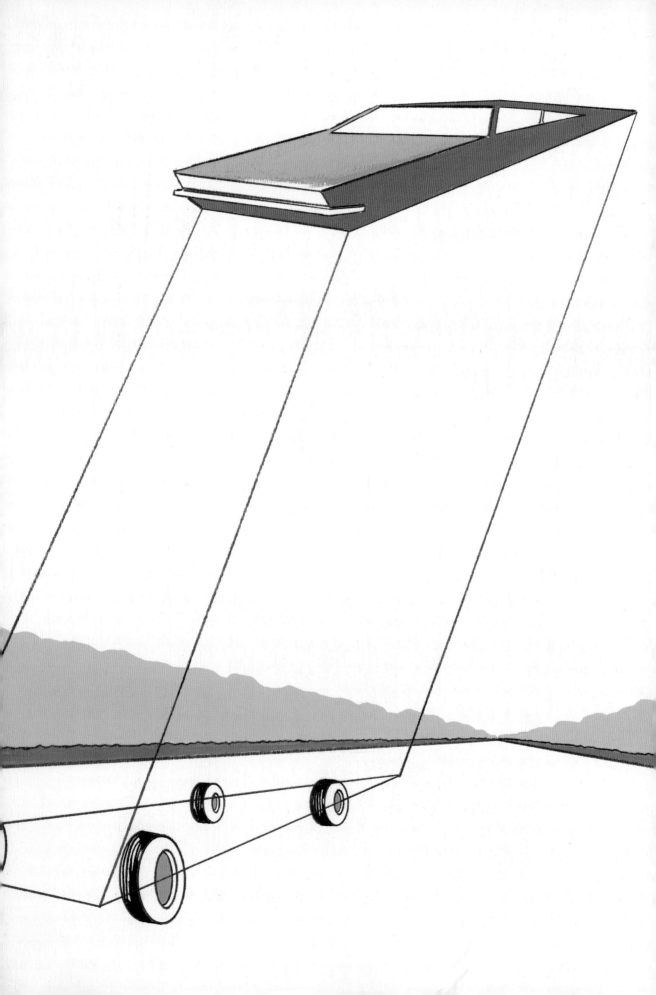

Touru Ogasawara
小笠原 徹

Media : Acrylic gouache / Crayon / Charcoal pen / Pencil / Color pencil
画材：アクリルガッシュ／クレヨン／チャコールペン／鉛筆／色鉛筆

Not only editorials, but also media in which I can express various approaches at home and abroad. I want to do various things, without caring about the size.

エディトリアルはもちろんのこと、国内外で、様々なアプローチを表現できる媒体。大小問わず、色々していきたいです。

1975年東京生まれ / 東京在住 / 東京工芸大学画像工学科卒

あ

See more artwork（バリエーションはこちら）>> http://www.pict-web.com/touru_ogasawara

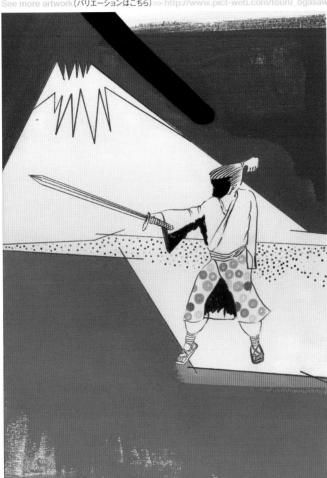

yoshiyuki okada
岡田 喜之

Media : Photoshop CS / Color pencil
画材 : Photoshop CS / 色鉛筆

I'm particularly interested in work related to fashion or sport, however I want to challenge myself in various fields to see how much I can express with my own style.

ファッションやスポーツ関係の仕事に特に興味をもっておりますが、自分のスタイルでどこまで表現できるかいろんな分野にチャレンジしてみたいです。

1978年埼玉県生まれ / 東京都在住 / セツ・モードセミナー卒

See more artwork (バリエーションはこちら) >> http://www.pict-web.com/yoshiyuki_okada

Sa-ko.

Sa-ko Okumura
おくむら さーこ

Media : Water color (Designers color)
画材 : 水彩 (Designers color)

I like cutting out and drawing the lifestyles of ordinary people, I'd like to try my hand at illustrations of catalogs connected to fashion, interiors. I'm also very interested in textile patterns.

特別ではなく、ある人たちのライフスタイルを切り取り描くことが好きで、インテリア・ファッション関連のカタログのイラストを手掛けてみたいです。またテキスタイルパターンにも大いに興味があります。

1977年東京生まれ / 神奈川在住 / 女子美術大学卒

See more artwork (バリエーションはこちら) >> http://www.pict-web.com/sa-ko_okumura

Isamu Gakiya
我喜屋 位瑳務

Media : Color pencil / Color ink / Collage
画材：色鉛筆 / カラーインク / コラージュ

I want to do any work that matches creations, but not strongly sticking to anything, CD or DVD jackets, posters of things like movies or theater, books, magazines, fliers, etc.

CD・DVDジャケット、映画・舞台などのポスター、書籍、雑誌、フライヤーなど強いこだわりはありませんが、作品に合った仕事であれば何でもやりたいです。

1974年沖縄県生まれ / 東京在住

See more artwork（バリエーションはこちら）>> http://www.pict-web.com/isamu_gakiya

065

midnight session

Yukako Kasai
笠井 由雅子

Media : Print / Paper cutting
画材：版画 / 切り絵

I would very much like to continue illustrations related to music, like CD jackets. From now on, I think I'd also like to create things like picture books.

今まで手掛けてきたCDジャケットなど、音楽に関するイラストは常に続けていきたいです。今後、絵本なども製作したいと思っています。

1974年大阪生まれ / 大阪在住

Peter Mayer

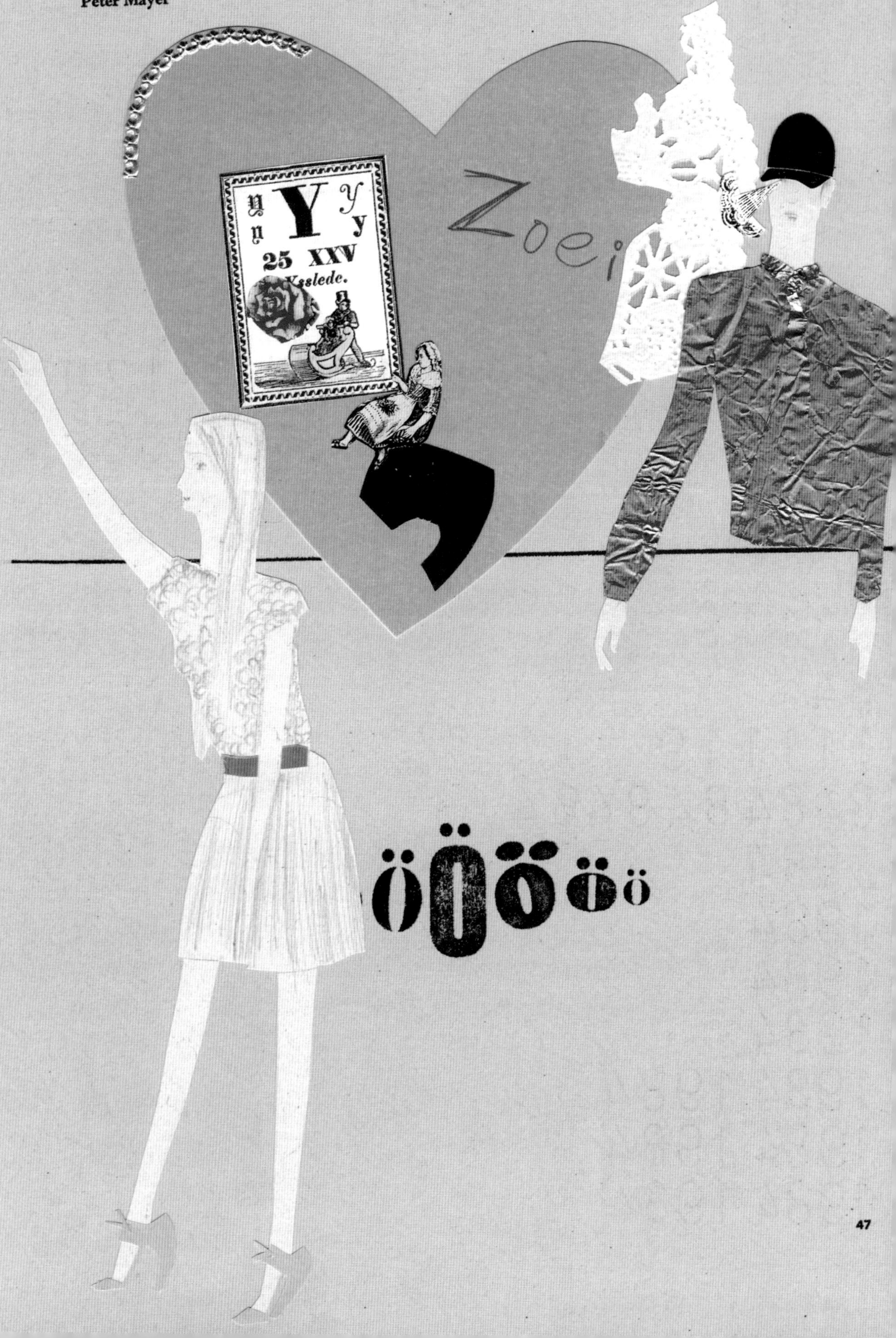

Hiroshi Kato
加藤 大

Media : Postercolor / Water color / Oil pastel / Cloth
画材：ポスターカラー / 水彩 / オイルパステル / 布

1972年愛知県生まれ / 東京在住 / 日本大学芸術学部美術学科卒

I've done lots of work with magazines, however from now on, I would like to try work in which I can send out signals to more people.

雑誌の仕事が多いですが、今後はTVCMやCDジャケットなど、より多くの人に向けて発信できる仕事をしてみたいです。

See more artwork（バリエーションはこちら）>> http://www.pict-web.com/hiroshi_kato

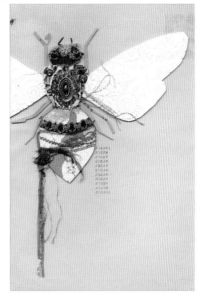

Yuko Kanatani
金谷 裕子

Media : Water color / Acrylic / Pencil /
Photoshop etc.
画材：水彩 / アクリル / 鉛筆 / Photoshopなど

I would like to try to do work where I create a rich
interpretation of the world through decorations for
things like shops and events, and art like images,
stage, photography, etc.

映像やステージ、写真などの美術や、ショップやイベントのデコ
レーションなどで濃厚に世界観を作る仕事がしてみたいです。

1975年兵庫県生まれ / 横浜市在住 / 成安造形大学卒

か

Miwa Kaburaki
鏑木 美和

Media : Water color / Photoshop 7.0
画材：水彩 / Photoshop 7.0

I want to challenge myself to express things that are not limited by two dimensions, like book design and music. I think that it would be good if I can make works which make the people who see them smile, and snuggle up to people's heart.

装丁・音楽関係など、また平面に限らない表現にも挑戦したい。見て頂いた人に微笑んでもらえるような心によりそえる作品を創っていけたらと思います。

東京都生まれ / 東京在住 / セツ・モードセミナー卒

か

See more artwork（バリエーションはこちら）>> http://www.pict-web.com/miwa_kaburaki

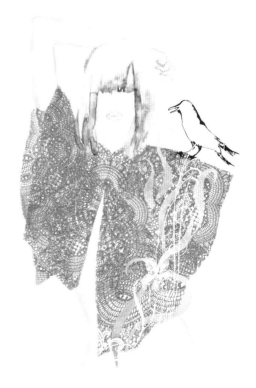

gumliens
ガムリアンズ

Media : Illustrator 8.0 / Photoshop 5.0 /
Acrylic gouache / Cray
画材 : Illustrator 8.0 / Photoshop 5.0 /
アクリルガッシュ / 石粉粘土

I hope I can do work in picture book making, music
CD jackets, and character design in things like
businesses and campaigns.

音楽CDジャケット、企業やキャンペーンなどのキャラクターデ
ザイン、絵本制作の仕事を希望しています。

ガム 太郎 1967年東京生まれ / 東京デザイナー学院卒
平山 ひとみ 1968年埼玉生まれ / 東京デザイナー学院卒

か

Midori Kawano
河野 未彩

Media : Photoshop CS2 / Illustrator CS2 / Pastel /
Acrylic / Pencil / Airbrush / Marker pen
画材 : Photoshop CS2 / Illustrator CS2 / パステル /
アクリル / 鉛筆 / エアーブラシ / コピック

Until now I've done a lot of art work related to music. However, I'm also interested in advertising that deals with product illustration or fashion illustration. I want to do work in the cosmetic advertising someday.

今まで音楽関連のアートワークが多かったのですが、商品イラストを扱う広告や、ファッションイラストにも興味があります。いつか化粧品広告がやってみたいのです！

1982年神奈川生まれ / 横浜在住 /
多摩美術大学プロダクトデザイン専攻卒

か

077

Fuko Kawamura
河村 ふうこ

Media : Photoshop CS2
画材 : Photoshop CS2

1968年東京生まれ / 東京在住 / 清泉女子大学英文科卒

I would like to draw pictures that make you feel comfortable. I think that I'd like to try various themes; fashion, interior, music...

心地よさを感じていただける絵を描いていきたいです。ファッションやインテリア、音楽……色々なテーマにトライしたいと思っています。

See more artwork（バリエーションはこちら）>> http://www.pict-web.com/fuko_kawamura

Mitsunari Kawamoto
川本 光成

Media : Illustrator 9.0
画材 : Illustrator 9.0

I think I want to answer a wide range of needs without being constrained by genre.

ジャンルを問わず幅広いニーズに答えていきたいと考えています。

1971年愛知県生まれ / 名古屋在住

See more artwork（バリエーションはこちら）>> http://www.pict-web.com/mitsunari_kawamoto

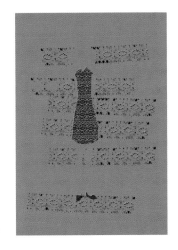

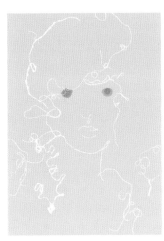

Mayumi Kishino
岸野 真弓

Media : Fabric / String
画材：布 / 糸

I make an effort to faithfully draw my world, and I'm happy if I can express things, like inconspicuously existing day by day, like noticing a stretched out string.

自分の世界に忠実素直に描けますよう努め、日々日常さりげなく存在していけるような、糸の連なりを目で触れるような、活躍ができれば幸せです。

1979年新潟県生まれ / 神戸在住 / 神戸ファッション専門学校卒

か

heisuke kitazawa or PCP

北沢 平祐

Media : Photoshop 7.0 / Cintiq 20wsx / Pencil / Eraser / Acrylic / Brush / Paper
画材 : Photoshop 7.0 / Cintiq 20wsx / 鉛筆 / 消しゴム / アクリル絵の具 / 筆 / 紙など

Album jackets of rock bands like the band "kururi," pop band's like the band "Of Montreal," and punk bands like the band, "Spitz's."

ロックバンド、くるりのアルバムジャケット。ポップバンド、of montrealのアルバムジャケット。パンクバンド、スピッツのアルバムジャケット。

1976年神奈川生まれ / 神奈川在住 /
cal state fullerton, Master of Illustrations

か

See more artwork (バリエーションはこちら) >> http://www.pict-web.com/heisuke_kitazawa

Jin Kitamura
北村 人

Media : Fusain / Crayon / Copy paper
画材：木炭 / クレヨン / コピー用紙

Now, I'm especially interested in animation. I think it's interesting if I can move my own work onto the web, etc.

現在は特に「アニメーション」に関心があります。ウェブなどで、自身の作品を動かすことが出来たら面白いと思います。

1981年東京生まれ / 神奈川在住 / 東海大学教養学部芸術学科卒

Toshiko Kimura
木村 敏子

Media : Photoshop CS / Illustrator CS /
Ballpoint pen / Water color / Acrylic
画材 : Photoshop CS / Illustrator CS / ボールペン /
水彩 / アクリル

I'd like to do work in movies. Aside from that I'd
like to move into illustration that concern life
directly like murals, apparel, fabric etc.

映画のお仕事をしてみたいです。その他にも壁画やアパレル、
ファブリックなど、生活のダイレクトに関わる部分でのイラスト
のお仕事を行ってみたいです。

1978年埼玉生まれ / 東京在住 / 創形美術学校ビジュアルデザイン科卒

See more artwork (バリエーションはこちら) >> http://www.pict-web.com/toshiko_kimura

NOBUO KUSUNOKI
楠 伸生

Media : Photoshop 5.02
画材 : Photoshop 5.02

I haven't had much experience up to this point working with books like novels, etc., so if I can do a lot of work in that area, I'll be happy.

これまで小説などの書籍のお仕事の経験が少なかったので、その辺りのお仕事が沢山出来ればうれしいです。

1958年大阪府生まれ / 東京在住

か

See more artwork (バリエーションはこちら) >> http://www.pict-web.com/nobuo_kusunoki

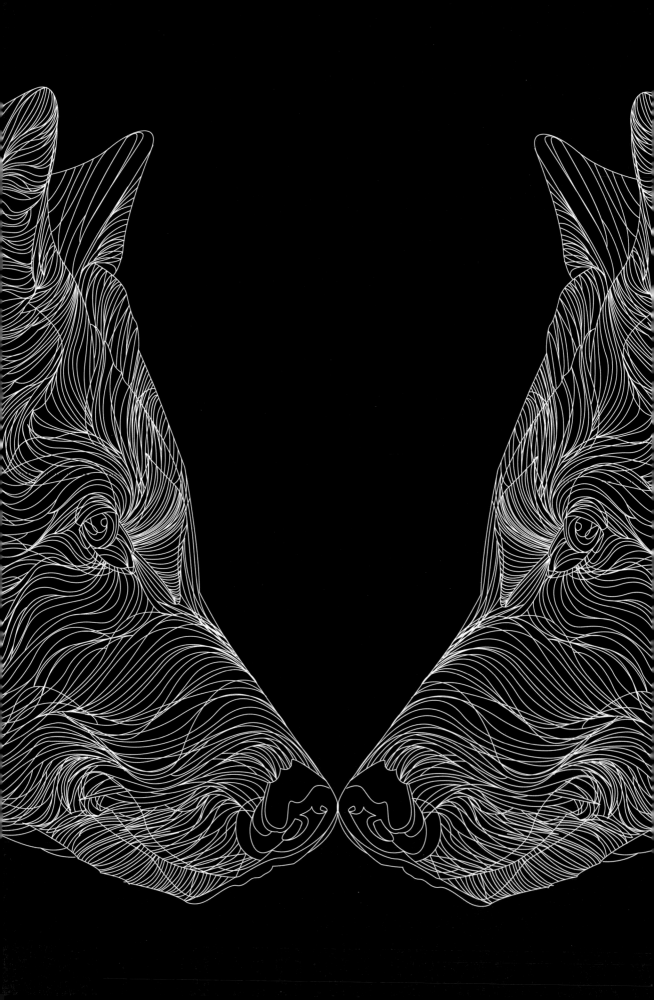

Kazuhiro Koizumi
古泉 和宏

Media : Photoshop CS / Illustrator CS etc.
画材 : Photoshop CS / Illustrator CS など

I want to do the kind of work in which I can create a good interaction between my design and work relating to food, clothing, and housing, and that remains for a long time.

衣食住に関わることと僕のデザインが良い相互作用をおこし長く残るような仕事がしたい。

1978年東京生まれ / 東京在住 / 千葉工業大学建築学科卒

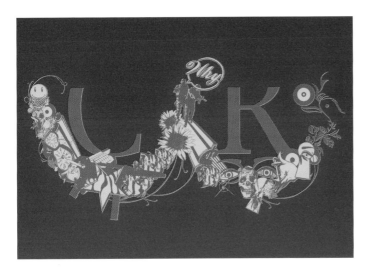

Yuki Koinuma
コイヌマ ユキ

Media : Photoshop CS2 / Water color / Crayon /
Color pencil / Pencil
画材：Photoshop CS2 / 水彩 / クレヨン / 色鉛筆 /
鉛筆

I think that it would be good if I can make things that spread the world of illustration, things like drawing pictures from stories, picture books, etc.

絵本など、お話から考えて絵を描いていくような、イラストの世界感が広がるようなものを作っていくことができたら良いなと思っています。

1980年神奈川生まれ / 埼玉在住 /
多摩美術大学グラフィックデザイン学科卒

か

See more artwork (バリエーションはこちら) >> http://www.pict-web.com/yuki_koinuma

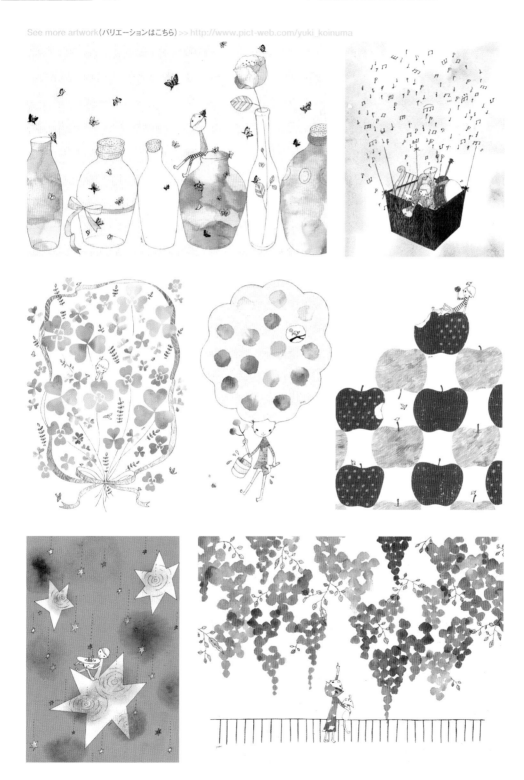

KO-ZOU
KO-ZOU

Media : Illustrator 10.0 / Photoshop 7.0
画材 : Illustrator 10.0 / Photoshop 7.0

Until now, I have been active mainly in two dimensions; like print media and the web, however, from now on, I'd also like to challenge myself in three dimensional things, or things like murals, unrelated to what I've done before.

今までは紙媒体やwebなど平面を中心に活動してきましたが、今後はそれ以外にも立体的なものや、壁画などに挑戦していきたいです。

1981年愛媛県生まれ / 神奈川在住 / 中京大学メディア学科卒

See more artwork（バリエーションはこちら）>> http://www.pict-web.com/ko-zou/

MASAFUMI KOTSUJI
小辻 雅史

Media : Photoshop CS2 / Illustrator CS2 /
Felt pen / Pencil
画材 : Photoshop CS2 / Illustrator CS2 / サインペン /
鉛筆

My works use lots of copy and paste, so I want to try to make some kind of textiles that can take advantage of those creations.

僕の作品はコピー＆ペーストを多様に使いますので、その作品の特性を生かした、テキスタイルなんかを作ってみたいです。

1976年東京都生まれ / 東京在住 / 創形美術学校卒

Aki Kobayashi
小林 晃

Media : Acrylic gouache / Ink / Photoshop 5.5
画材：アクリルガッシュ / インク / Photoshop 5.5

1978年栃木生まれ / 東京在住 / セツ・モードセミナー卒

I'd like to try to do work having to do with music; CD jackets, etc. I think that it would be great if I could draw pictures that you can hear the sound of.

CDジャケットなど音楽に関連するお仕事をしてみたいです。音が聴こえてくるような絵を描いていけたら素敵だなと思っております。

か

See more artwork（バリエーションはこちら）>> http://www.pict-web.com/aki_kobayashi

Hiromitsu Kobayashi
小林 宏光

Media : Acrylic gouache / Color pencil
画材：アクリルガッシュ / 色鉛筆

1977年神奈川生まれ / 神奈川在住 / イラストレーション青山塾卒

I'd like to try my hand at things like book design, editorial design, or advertising work, etc.

装丁などエディトリアルや広告の仕事なども手がけてみたいです。

See more artwork（バリエーションはこちら）>> http://www.pict-web.com/hiromitsu_kobayashi

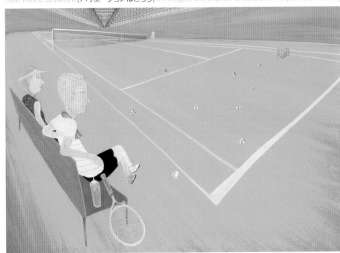

Komtena
komtena

Media : Pencil / Pen / Acrylic / Photoshop CS /
Illustrator 8.0
画材：鉛筆 / ペン / アクリル / Photoshop CS /
Illustrator 8.0

I want to work in every field; centered around print media. Basically I want to try my hand at any work that asks me to push me to my limit.

紙媒体を中心にあらゆる分野の仕事をしたい。基本的に依頼された仕事は可能な限り手がけていきたいです。

1978年神奈川生まれ / 神奈川在住 /
多摩美術大学グラフィックデザイン科卒

See more artwork（バリエーションはこちら）>> http://www.pict-web.com/komtena

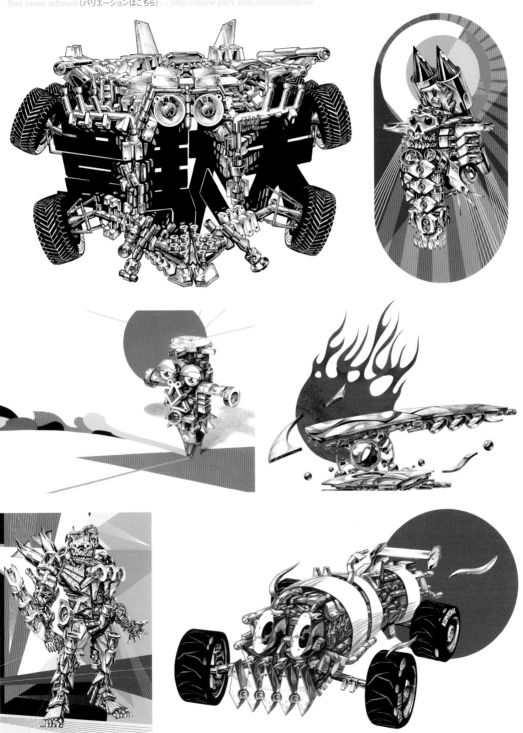

Yusuke Saitoh
サイトウ ユウスケ

Media : Photoshop CS / Painter X.5
画材 : Photoshop CS / Painter X.5

I would like to do the kind of work that can some-how move people the moment they see it. And, I would also like to collaborate with a lot of other creators in different kinds of media.

作品を見た瞬間に何らかの感動を与えられるような仕事をしたいです。そしてメディアを越えてたくさんのクリエイターたちとコラボレートしたいです。

1978年神奈川生まれ / 東京都在住 /
バンタンデザイン研究所ビジュアル学部卒

See more artwork（バリエーションはこちら）>> http://www.pict-web.com/yusuke_saitoh

さ

NAO SAKAMOTO
坂本 奈緒

Media : Ballpoint pen / Photoshop
画材：ボールペン / Photoshop

Of course I'd like to work on magazines, but also book design.

雑誌はもちろんですが、装幀のお仕事をしたいです。

1979年北海道生まれ / 東京都在住 /
コム・イラストレーターズ・スタジオ修了

See more artwork（バリエーションはこちら）>> http://www.pict-web.com/nao_sakamoto

さ

Ryo Sakuma
佐久間 遼

Media : Photoshop CS2 / Illustrator CS2
画材 : Photoshop CS2 / Illustrator CS2

I'm doing mainly personal work, and I'm also active as a graphic and web designer. I'd like to move to exhibit in various places.

パーソナルワークを中心に、グラフィック・WEBデザイナーとしても活動。様々な場所で展示をしていきたいです。

1982年北海道生まれ / 東京在住 / 駒沢大学経済学部卒

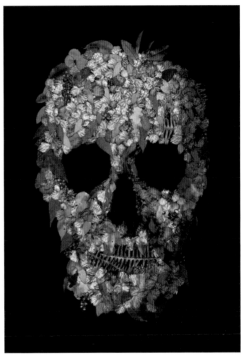

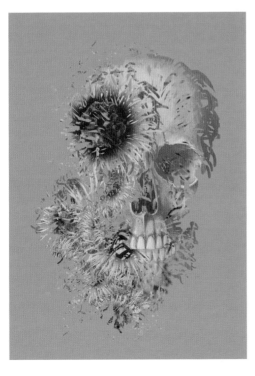

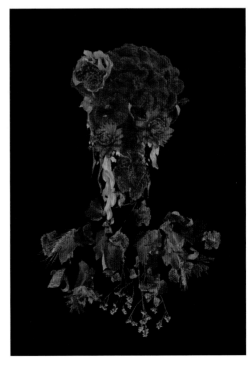

The Skull Dezain
THE SKULL DEZAIN

The matter I'm working on at this moment is the most important, the time when I don't have any work I play games with all my effort, so there isn't any room for using my brain for things related to matters I haven't seen.

今現在手掛けている案件が一番大事で、且つ、お仕事が無い時間は全力でゲームをしていますので、まだ見ぬ案件に関して脳ミソを廻す余裕はありません。

Media : Illustrator 8.0 / Photoshop 8.0
画材 : Illustrator 8.0 / Photoshop 8.0

2002年より活動開始 / 兵庫在住 / 県立高校卒

Shunsuke Satake
サタケ シュンスケ

Media : Acrylic / Pencil / Photoshop CS2 /
Illustrator CS2
画材 : アクリル / 鉛筆 / Photoshop CS2 /
Illustrator CS2

I want to try to challenge myself in work that asks
for individual characteristics through what I draw,
like characters of things like businesses, groups,
and events, also picture books, etc.

企業・団体・イベントなどのキャラクターや絵本など、描くものに
より個性が求められるようなお仕事に挑戦してみたいです。

1981年大阪府生まれ / 神戸在住 /
神戸デザイナー学院グラフィックデザイン学科卒

See more artwork（バリエーションはこちら）>> http://www.pict-web.com/shunsuke_satake

ASAMI SATO
サトウ アサミ

Media : Chinese ink / Acrylic
画材：墨 / アクリル絵の具

I want to carefully continue my artwork inside the space that I've built up to now. I think it would be fun to work with the world in other genres like music, theater, etc.

今までやってきた空間の中でのアートワークは大切に続けていきたい。音楽、お芝居など別ジャンルの世界とご一緒できたら楽しいだろうなと思います。

1977年札幌生まれ / 札幌在住 / 札幌大谷短期大学デザイン科卒

See more artwork（バリエーションはこちら）>> http://www.pict-web.com/asami_sato

さ

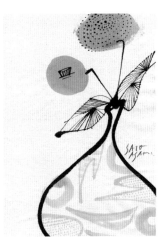

AYUMI SATO
さとう あゆみ

Media : Photoshop CS3
画材 : Photoshop CS3

I'd be happy if I can do the kind of work where I can express dignified beauty and female clarity. I want to challenge myself in new work as I make good use of my experience so far.

女性の透明感や凛とした美しさを表現できるようなお仕事ができれば嬉しいです。今までの経験を生かしつつ、新しいことにチャレンジしていきたいです。

長野県生まれ / 東京在住 / 短大卒

See more artwork（バリエーションはこちら）>> http://www.pict-web.com/ayumi_sato

Yohei Sano
佐野 洋平

Media : Board / Canvas board / Acrylic / Pen /
Photoshop 7.0
画材 : 板 / キャンバスボード / アクリル絵の具 / ペン /
Photoshop 7.0

I like traveling, so I would like to try work associated with travel. I'd like to draw pictures that have curiosity.

旅をするのが好きなので、旅にまつわるお仕事をしてみたいです。好奇心をもって絵を描いていきたいです。

1979年三重県生まれ / 三重県在住 /
インターナショナルアカデミーバレットクラブイラスト教室卒

See more artwork (バリエーションはこちら) >> http://www.pict-web.com/yohei_sano

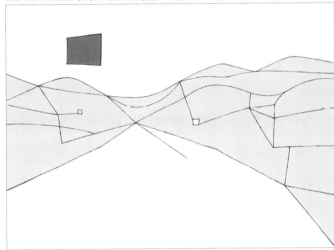

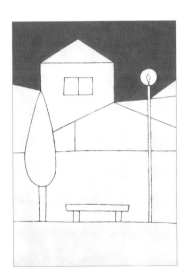

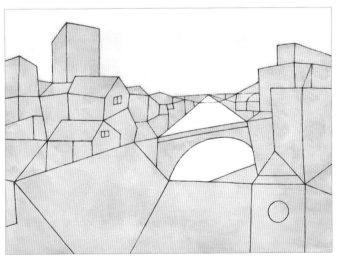

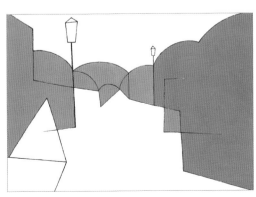

Izumi Shiokawa

塩川 いづみ

Media : Acrylic / Pencil
画材：アクリル / 鉛筆

1980年長野県生まれ / 東京在住 /
多摩美術大学グラフィックデザイン科卒

I'd like to do work with people in a variety of fields both in Japan, and abroad.

日本でも海外でも様々な分野の方とお仕事をしてみたいです。

Hattaro Shinano
信濃 八太郎

Media : Chinese ink / Brush / Cutter / Photoshop CS
画材：墨 / 筆 / カッター / Photoshop CS

I've been producing simple movies that connect pictures, so I think that I want to try to do advertising work like commercials where I can use them.

絵をつないだ簡単なMovieの制作も行っているので、それを使ったCMなど、広告の仕事をやってみたいと思ってます。

1974年千葉生まれ / 東京在住 / 日本大学芸術学部卒

さ

柴田 ケイコ

I think I want to be useful for somebody's something, through work in a wide range of media, not limited by small surroundings.

小さい範囲にとどまらず、いろいろなあらゆるメディアの範囲で
お仕事をし、誰かの何かの役に立ちたいと思う。

Media : Oil pastel / Color pencil / Craft paper /
Collage
画材：オイルパステル / 色鉛筆 / クラフト紙 / コラージュ

1973年高知県生まれ / 高知在住 /
奈良芸術短期大学ビジュアルデザイン科卒

See more artwork（バリエーションはこちら）>> http://www.pict-web.com/keiko_shibata

Noriko Shimizu
清水 宣子

Media : Acrylic
画材：アクリル絵の具

I like clothes, so work related to fashion (store image visuals, textiles, etc.). I'd like to make picture books that attach a story to my pictures.

洋服が好きなのでファッションに関わるお仕事（店舗のイメージビジュアルやテキスタイルなど）を。それと自分の絵に物語をつけて絵本を作りたいです。

1972年石川県金沢市生まれ / 東京在住 / パレットクラブ卒

See more artwork（バリエーションはこちら）>> http://www.pict-web.com/noriko_shimizu

さ

Masashi Shimizu
清水 将司 (gaimgraphics)

Media : Illustrator CS / Photoshop CS /
Several Pen / Paper
画材 : Illustrator CS / Photoshop CS / あらゆるペン /
拾った紙

I find it more rewarding to work with clients who I can keep in touch with after finishing the work, rather than just the work itself. I don't think that it matters whether that work is large, small, domestic, or international. I want to have excitement in my work.

仕事だけじゃなく、その後もつき合っていけるようなクライアントさんとの仕事こそ、やりがいを見いだせます。そこに大きい仕事、小さい仕事、国内、海外もないと思ってます。仕事でワクワクしたいです。

1980年栃木生まれ / 東京在住 / 東京造形大学造形学部デザイン学科卒

さ

Yoichi Shimoda
下田 洋一

Media : Water color / Paper cutout
画材：水彩絵具 / 切絵

I've been drawing not only human figures, but also nature such as flowers, but recently I feel as if it's interesting to abstractly cut out forms of dishes, etc.

人物以外にも、花をはじめ自然を描いていますが、最近は器などのフォルムを抽象的に切り取ることがおもしろいと感じています。

1972年東京生まれ / 東京在住 / セツ・モードセミナー卒

さ

See more artwork（バリエーションはこちら）>> http://www.pict-web.com/yoichi_shimoda

Jun Watanabe
Jun Watanabe

Media : Illustrator 10 / Photoshop CS /
FASKOLOR
画材 : Illustrator 10 / Photoshop CS / FASKOLOR

Branding work either with a single company, or
with an organizational group.

ひとつの会社もしくは組織体をブランディングしていくこと。

1977年新潟県生まれ / 千葉在住 / 東京デザイナー学院卒

SHOHEI TAKASAKI
ショウヘイ タカサキ

Art direction for great musicians, collaboration with artists who make great clothes.

素晴らしい音楽アーティストのアート・ディレクション、素晴らしい洋服アーティストとのコラボレーション。

Media : Pencil / G-Pen / Permanent marker etc.
画材：鉛筆 / Gペン / 油性マジックなど

埼玉県生まれ / 東京都在住

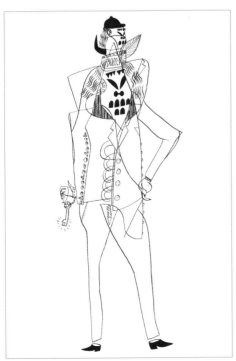

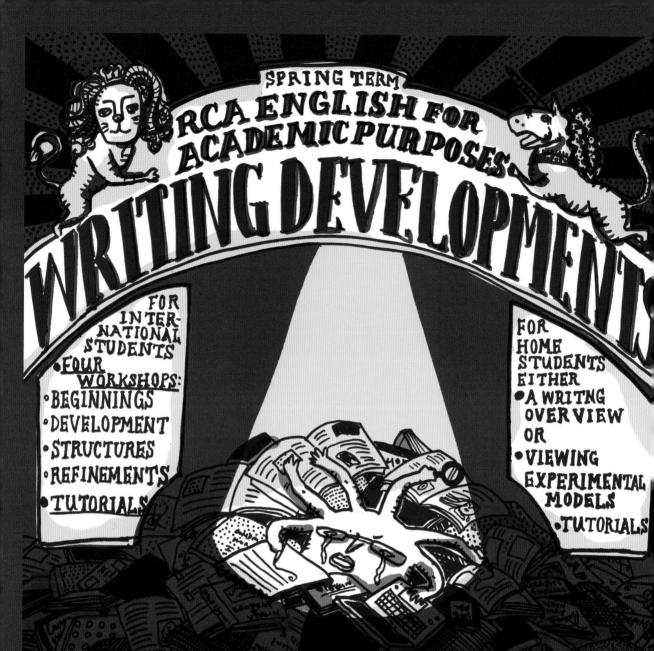

SPRING TERM
RCA ENGLISH FOR ACADEMIC PURPOSES

WRITING DEVELOPMENTS

FOR INTERNATIONAL STUDENTS
- FOUR WORKSHOPS:
- BEGINNINGS
- DEVELOPMENT
- STRUCTURES
- REFINEMENTS
- TUTORIALS

FOR HOME STUDENTS EITHER
- A WRITING OVERVIEW OR
- VIEWING EXPERIMENTAL MODELS
- TUTORIALS

HOW TO ACCESS:
- EAP. INTER-NET
- EAP. RCADE
- VIA ADMINISTRATORS
- VIA PHONE. EMAIL FROM JANUARY 21st

SEE ALSO RCADE EAP RESOURCES (MADD)

HARRIET EDWARDS
SIMON KING

Haruka Shinji
進士 遙

Media : Screen print / Photoshop CS / Pen / Ink
画材：スクリーンプリント / Photoshop CS / ペン / インク

I prefer paper itself more than webpages or moving images, so I would like to make something I can touch and hold, just like posters, book cover illustrations and toys.

web や映像よりも紙が好きなので、ポスター、本の装丁、おもちゃなど、手に取ることのできるものを作る仕事ができればと思っています。

1984年千葉県生まれ / 上海育ち / ロンドン在住 /
英国王立芸術大学院在籍

Hidehito Shinno
新納 英仁

Media : Photoshop CS / Illustrator CS
画材 : Photoshop CS / Illustrator CS

Presently, I'm interested in textile design, so I want to try my hand at both merchandise and clothes that you can somehow enjoy, through the pattern which uses my own character or icon.

現在テキスタイルデザインに興味がありますので、自分のキャラクターやアイコンを用いたパターンで何か楽しい洋服や雑貨を手がけてみたいです。

1981年愛知県生まれ / 神奈川県在住 /
名古屋造形デザイン専門学校グラフィックデザイン科卒

さ

Mihoko Seki
関 美穂子

Media : Paints
画材 : 顔料

I want to make picture books, book illustrations, cover art, etc. I'd like to try to continue work related to fabric like yukatas (traditional Japanese summer clothes) etc. taking advantage of dying techniques.

本の装画や、挿絵、絵本などをしたいです。染色の技法をいかして手ぬぐい、浴衣など繊維関係も引き続きしていきたいです。

1980年生まれ / 神奈川県横浜市出身 / 京都在住 /
別府大学短期大学部(初等教育科)卒

See more artwork(バリエーションはこちら)>> http://www.pict-web.com/mihoko_seki

Daisuke Soshiki
祖敷 大輔

Media : Oil pastel / Color pencil / Dermato graph / Acrylic
画材 : オイルパステル / 色鉛筆 / ダーマトグラフ / アクリル

I think that I'd like to draw in a medium that you can touch, such as magazines, books, etc.

雑誌、書籍など、見る人の手に触れられるメディアで描きたいと思っています。

1979年山口県生まれ / 東京在住 / 武蔵野美術大学卒

さ

See more artwork (バリエーションはこちら) >> http://www.pict-web.com/daisuke_soshiki

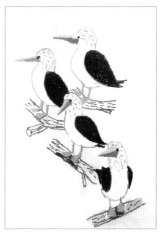

145

Takashi Taima
泰間 敬視

Media : Plywood / Varnish / Gesso
画材：シナベニヤ / 水性ニス / ジェッソ

1971年大阪府生まれ / 東京在住

Magazines, cover art, advertising, etc. Especially work involving music. CD jackets, posters, etc. Internet, TV, commercials, etc.

雑誌や装画や広告や。特に音楽関連の仕事を。CDジャケットやポスターや。webやTVやCMや。

See more artwork（バリエーションはこちら）>> http://www.pict-web.com/takashi_taima

Hiroko Takashino
高篠 裕子

Media : Water color / Acrylic gouache / Ink / Pencil
画材：水彩 / ガッシュ / インク / 鉛筆

I'll be happy if I can come across the kind of work where the things I draw are connected with new discoveries that even I can't imagine.

描いたものが自分でも想像のつかない新しい発見に繋がるようなお仕事にめぐり合えたら嬉しいです。

1983年東京生まれ / 東京在住 / セツ・モードセミナー卒

See more artwork（バリエーションはこちら）>> http://www.pict-web.com/hiroko_takashino

た

Takeuma
タケウマ

Media : Pen / Photoshop 6.0
画材 : ペン / Photoshop 6.0

Work where designers or editors and I can bounce ideas off each other.

デザイナーや編集者とアイデアを出し合える仕事。

京都在住 / 京都工芸繊維大学造形工学科卒

Yoshi Tajima
田嶋 吉信

Media : Pencil / Pen / Ink / Photoshop CS3 /
Illustrator CS3 / Photoshop 5.5 / Illustrator 8.0
画材 : 鉛筆 / ペン / インク / Photoshop CS3 /
Illustrator CS3 / Photoshop 5.5 / Illustrator 8.0

Things that you can feel the smell or the air of,
things in which the person seeing them imagines a
fantasy. I want to be active in fashion, music, life,
etc., regardless of the country.

空気や香りを感じてもらえるようなもの、見る人がファンタジー
を想うようなもの。ファッション〜音楽〜ライフなど国内外を問
わず活動したい。

1969年千葉県生まれ / 東京都在住 /
AIU in London, Commercial Art専攻 BA卒

See more artwork（バリエーションはこちら）>> http://www.pict-web.com/yoshi_tajima

Michiko Tachimoto
(colobockle)
立本 倫子 (コロボックル)

Media : Photoshop 6.0 / Water color / Acrylic /
Pencil / Crayon
画材：Photoshop 6.0 / 水彩 / アクリル / 鉛筆 / クレヨン

Including picture books, design of things familiar to
children, like magazines, images, and general merchandise for children. I want to try my hand at mul-
timedia aimed at children.

絵本をはじめ、子ども向けの雑誌や映像や雑貨など子どもた
ちの身近なモノたちをデザインし、子ども向けのマルチメディア
を手がけていきたいです。

1976年石川生まれ / 神奈川在住 / 大阪芸術大学デザイン学科卒

See more artwork（バリエーションはこちら）>> http://www.pict-web.com/michiko_tachimoto

Colobockle

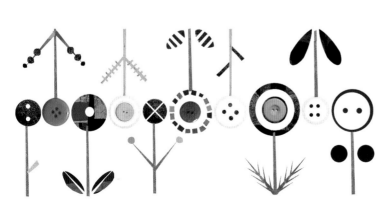

colobockle

Sae Tachimori
日月 沙絵

Media : Pen / Painter 8
画材：ペン / Painter 8

I'd like to be widely active in advertising, album jackets, book covers, etc. Also, I'm interested in sponsoring creations in image related fields like TV commercials, music promotion, etc.

広告、ジャケット、書籍カバーなど幅広く活動していきたいです。またTVCMや音楽プロモなど、映像分野への作品提供にも興味があります。

1984年大阪府生まれ / 大阪在住 / 京都市立芸術大学漆工科卒

See more artwork（バリエーションはこちら）>> http://www.pict-web.com/sae_tachimori

Mariko Tanaka
田中 麻里子

Media : Pencil / Marker pen / Acrylic / Canvas
画材：鉛筆 / アルコールマーカー / アクリル /
キャンバス

In the fashion industry, like the design of t-shirts, bags, etc. CD jackets, book illustration. Also textiles, wrapping paper design, etc.

Tシャツやバッグの絵柄などのファッションの分野や、CDジャケット・書籍の挿画。また、テキスタイルやラッピングペーパーの模様など。

1979年宮城生まれ / 東京在住

See more artwork（バリエーションはこちら）>> http://www.pict-web.com/mariko_tanaka

159

Toshifumi Tanabu
田名部 敏文

Media : Photoshop CS2 / Illustrator CS2
画材 : Photoshop CS2 / Illustrator CS2

Until now, I've worked on advertising, cigarette packaging (Noire Brand), etc. I want to expand my work into packaging, and products that you can actually pick up and enjoy.

これまで広告や煙草「ノアール」のパッケージなどを手掛けました。実際に手に取って喜んで頂ける商品やパッケージのお仕事を広げたいです。

1976年青森県生まれ / 東京在住 / 法政大学経済学部卒

た

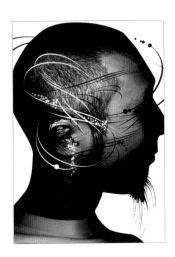

danny
danny

Media : Color pencil / Craypas
画材：色鉛筆 / ソフトクレパス

I think it would be good if I can mainly do work having to do with ecology and the environment. Aside from that I'm also interested in music and magazines.

エコや環境に関係する仕事を主にやっていけたらいいな、と思います。その他にも音楽や、雑誌にも興味があります。

1987年岡山生まれ / 京都在住 /
京都精華大学デザイン学部イラストレーションコース在籍

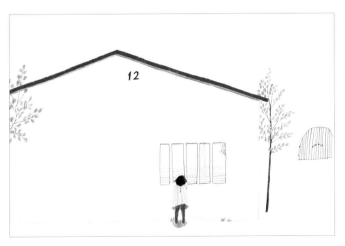

Tomonori Taniguchi
谷口 智則

Media : Acrylic / Chinese ink
画材：アクリル絵の具 / 墨

I want to publish picture books about different countries of the world, hold exhibitions in those countries, touch many people from children to adults, then I want people to read my picture books.

世界中の国々で絵本を出版し、その国々で展覧会を開催し、大人から子どもまでたくさんの人々と触れあい、そして自分の絵本を読んでもらいたい。

1978年生まれ / 大阪在住 / 金沢美術工芸大学日本画専攻卒

See more artwork（バリエーションはこちら）>> http://www.pict-web.com/tomonori_taniguchi

た

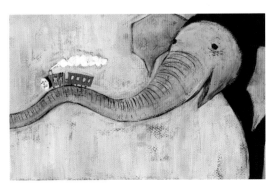

Kayo Tamura
タムラ カヨ

Media : Ballpoint pen / Pen / Marker pen /
Photoshop / Collage
画材：ボールペン / ペン / コピック / Photoshop /
コラージュ

I think that I want to challenge myself in anything
that is interesting. I want to try my hand at apparel
work like clothing illustration, etc.

面白いことならなんでも挑戦したいと思っています。洋服のイラ
ストなどのアパレルの仕事を手がけてみたいです。

1982年群馬県出身 / 東京在住

た

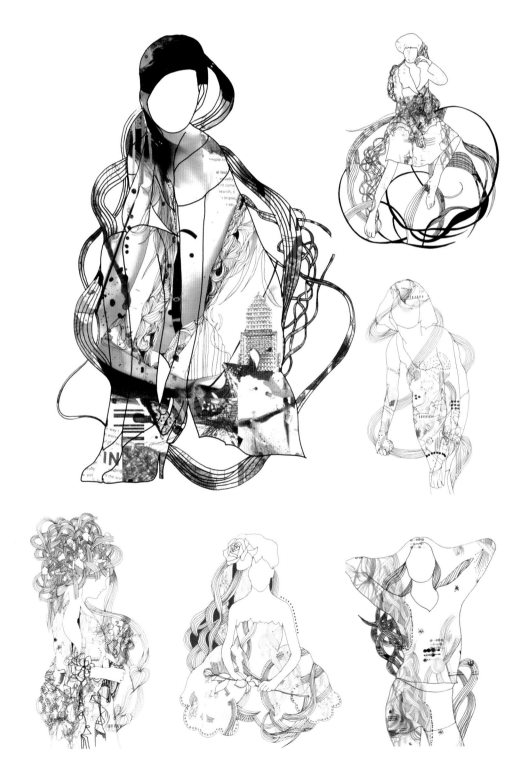

chinatsu
chinatsu

Media : Photoshop / Acrylic / Pencil
画材 : Photoshop / アクリル / 鉛筆

Now, I'd like to do work that fascinates me that I've dreamed about since I was young like fashion, etc., and if I can dig deeper, I'd like to do work that deeply moves people's hearts.

今は幼い頃からの憧れのファッションなど魅せる仕事を、自分に深みがもっとでてたら、人の心に深く伝わる仕事をしたいです。

鹿児島生まれ

See more artwork (バリエーションはこちら) >> http://www.pict-web.com/chinatsu

YOU

THANK DAD!

Keiko Tsuji
辻 恵子

Media : Scissors / Pen / Glue /
Paper (Printed material etc.)
画材：はさみ / ペン / のり / 紙（印刷物など）

I usually show paper cutouts at my exhibitions, but also I enjoy wood printing recently. I am interested in lettering design, calligraphy and making picture book as well.

個展では切り絵作品をお見せすることが多いですが、最近は木版画も楽しんで創っています。また、切り文字や手書き文字、絵本づくりにも興味があります。

1975年東京生まれ / 東京在住 / 文化学院文学科卒

See more artwork（バリエーションはこちら）>> http://www.pict-web.com/keiko_tsuji

shobu tsuchiya
土谷 尚武

Media : Photoshop 7.0 / Illustrator 10.0
画材 : Photoshop 7.0 / Illustrator 10.0

I don't have a field I'm stuck to or anything special that I want to try my hand at. Rather, I want to do work with people who can share their interpretation of the world, and their sense of values.

特別に手がけてみたいという固執した分野はありません。それよりも価値観や世界観を共有できる人間と仕事がしたいです。

1963年アルゼンチン生まれ / 東京在住 /
日本大学芸術学部デザイン学科卒

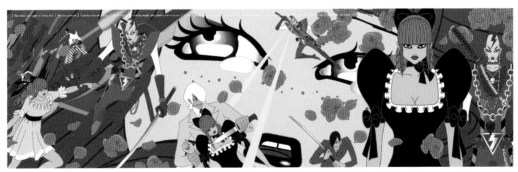

tupera tupera
ツペラツペラ

Media : Color paper / Acrylic / Silk screen
画材：色紙 / アクリル絵の具 / シルクスクリーン

Until now, I have made products with various expressions. I want to move to express work that I feel interested in each and every time; from two dimensions, to three dimensions and images, regardless of the medium or the technique.

これまで様々な表現で作品を創ってきました。平面から立体、映像まで、媒体や技法に関わらず、その都度おもしろいと感じた事を表現していきたいです。

亀山 達矢 1976年三重県生まれ / 東京都在住 / 武蔵野美術大学油絵学科卒
中川 敦子 1978年東京都生まれ / 東京都在住 / 多摩美術大学染色学科卒

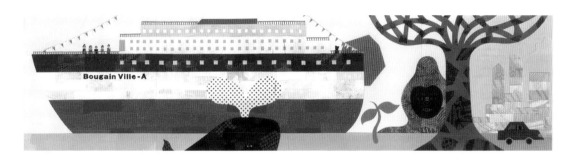

た

175

tetsuro oh!no
tetsuro oh!no

Media : Illustrator 10 / Photoshop CS2
画材 : Illustrator 10 / Photoshop CS2

I want to try my hand at things like wall murals, not so much concrete situation illustration, but something like color configuration or patterned works.

具体的なシチュエーションイラストと言うより、より色彩構成的というか、柄的な作品であったり、壁画のようなものも手がけてみたい。

仙台生まれ / 東京在住

See more artwork（バリエーションはこちら）>> http://www.pict-web.com/tetsuro_ohno

TOKUMA
TOKUMA

Media : Illustrator CS2
画材 : Illustrator CS2

Quiet relaxing work. Book design for novels and murals.

小説などの本の装丁や、壁画。静かで落ち着いた仕事。

1973年新潟県生まれ / 東京都在住 /
広告デザイン専門学校グラフィックデザイン科卒

See more artwork (バリエーションはこちら) >> http://www.pict-web.com/tokuma

Haruka Toshimitsu
利光 春華

Media : Color pencil / Pen / Acrylic / Croquis pad / Photoshop CS
画材：色鉛筆 / ペン / アクリル / クロッキー帳 / Photoshop CS

Collaborating on book design, product packaging, fashion branding. I want to actively challenge myself in anything if there are new projects beyond the framework of illustration.

装丁、製品パッケージ、ファッションブランドとのコラボレート。イラストレーションの枠を超えた新しい企画があれば何事にも前向きに挑戦してみたい。

1983年大分生まれ / 埼玉在住 / 東洋美術学校グラフィックデザイン科卒

た

Hideki Toda
戸田 英毅

Media : STRATA 3D CX / Photoshop CS2
画材 : STRATA 3D CX / Photoshop CS2

Closer to a dream rather than a work, I'd actually like to try to make figures, objects, architecture, furniture, etc. into three dimensional works, making use of 3D data.

仕事というより夢に近いんですが、3Dデータを生かしてフィギア・オブジェ・建築・家具など作品を実際に立体化してみたいですね。

1959年広島生まれ / 東京在住 / 多摩美術大学グラフィックデザイン科卒

See more artwork（バリエーションはこちら）>> http://www.pict-web.com/hideki_toda

た

MIZUKI TOTORI
戸取 瑞樹

Media : Color pencil / Silk screen / Aftereffect /
Illustrator / Photoshop
画材：色鉛筆 / シルクスクリーン / Aftereffect /
Illustrator / Photoshop

Business commercial identity, public visual identity, sign planning, characters on children's TV programs. TV animation, movies.

企業CI、公共VI、サイン計画、子供TV番組のキャラクター、
TVアニメ、映画。

1973年東京生まれ / 東京稼働 / 武蔵野美術大学デザイン学部卒

た

Yoh Nagao
長尾 洋

Media : Acrylic / Pencil / Felt pen / Mechanical pencil / Collage / Illustrator 10 / Photoshop 6
画材：アクリル / 鉛筆 / サインペン / シャープペン / コラージュ / Illustrator 10 / Photoshop 6

I want to do work related to music which involves working with specific musicians, from print media like CD jackets to video clip images, animation, etc.

特定のミュージシャンと組んでCDジャケットなどの紙媒体から、ビデオクリップの映像やアニメーションなどにまで絡む様な音楽関係の仕事をしてみたい。

1981年神奈川生まれ / 愛知県在住 / 名古屋造形大学デザイン科卒

な

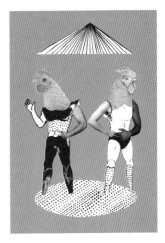

Gaku Nakagawa
中川 学

Media : Pencil / Illustrator CS / Photoshop CS
画材：鉛筆 / Illustrator CS / Photoshop CS

1966年東京生まれ / 京都在住 / 仏教大学文学部仏教学科卒

Collaboration with traditional artisans on book design / cover art, book illustrations, magazines, animation, and wood engraving, etc.

装丁画、挿絵、アニメーション、雑貨、木版画など伝統的な職人さんたちとのコラボレーション。

See more artwork (バリエーションはこちら) >> http://www.pict-web.com/gaku_nakagawa

な

Kazuhiro Nakazato
仲里 カズヒロ

Media : Illustrator CS / Photoshop CS
画材 : Illustrator CS / Photoshop CS

Until now, I've absorbed a wide range of senses through electronic media. Even in magazines or the net, I want to express the essence of loveliness and ticklishness.

これまでに電波媒体でバラエティな感覚をたくさん吸収してきました。雑誌やネットでも、そのエッセンス『可愛げ』『くすぐり感覚』を表現していきたいです。

1964年大阪生まれ / 大阪在住

See more artwork(バリエーションはこちら)>> http://www.pict-web.com/kazuhiro_nakazato

Makoto Nakazawa
ナカザワ マコト

Media : Photoshop 8.0 / Illustrator 10 / Painter X /
Water color / Pencil / Ballpoint pen
画材 : Photoshop 8.0 / Illustrator 10 / Painter X /
水彩絵具 / 鉛筆 / ボールペン

Advertising, magazines, book design, cover art,
picture books, comic books, CD/DVD jackets,
product packaging, the internet, images.

広告、雑誌、装丁、装画、絵本、漫画、CD・DVDジャケット、
商品パッケージ、Web、映像。

1977年長野県生まれ / 東京在住 / 広島市立大学芸術学部油絵専攻卒

See more artwork (バリエーションはこちら) >> http://www.pict-web.com/makoto_nakazawa

193

Kana Nakajima
中島 香奈

Media : Pencil / Water color pencil
画材：鉛筆 / 水彩色鉛筆

I think it would be great if I had an opportunity to send some kind of message to protect animals and the environment through my illustration.

動物や環境の保護にイラストを通して何かしらメッセージを送れるような機会があればと思っています。

1968年生まれ / 京都在住 / 大阪モード学園メイクアップスタイリスト科卒

See more artwork（バリエーションはこちら）>> http://www.pict-web.com/kana_nakajima

な

Rie Nakajima
中島 梨絵

Media : Water color / Acrylic gouache
画材：水彩 / アクリルガッシュ

I think that I want to do the kind of work that widens my expression, mainly book binding art, magazine illustration, etc.

書籍の装幀画や雑誌の挿絵などを中心に、表現の幅を広げていけるような仕事をしていきたいと思っています。

1981年滋賀県生まれ / 東京在住 / 京都精華大学マンガ学科卒

Ryoji Nakajima
中島 良二

Media : Acrylic / Oil pastel
画材：アクリル / オイルパステル

1976年大阪府生まれ / 大阪在住 / 神戸大学発達科学部卒

I think if I could communicate with lots of people through a wide range of work without constraints.

枠を設けず、幅広いお仕事を通じて、たくさんの方々とかかわり合うことができればと思っています。

See more artwork(バリエーションはこちら) >> http://www.pict-web.com/ryoji_nakajima

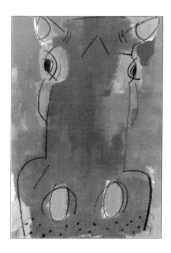

Yu Nagaba
長場 雄

Media : Photoshop CS / Illustrator CS / Sign pen / Pencil / Color pencil
画材 : Photoshop CS / Illustrator CS / サインペン / 鉛筆 / 色鉛筆

I want to draw advertising illustrations because I want lots of people to see my work. Also I want to challenge myself to make picture books, and produce clothes and bags from original cloth.

より多くの人に見てもらいたいので、広告のイラストを描いてみたい。他にはオリジナルの生地で服やバッグ制作、絵本にも挑戦してみたい。

1976年東京生まれ / 東京在住 / 東京造形大学デザイン学科卒

な

Yoco Nagamiya
永宮 陽子

Media : Water color / Pen / Ink
画材 : 水彩 / ペン / インク

Collaboration with other creators, like fashion brand product projects, TV commercial imaging, etc.

ファッションブランドなどの商品企画や、TVCMの映像化など。
他クリエイターの方々とのコラボレーションなど。

1973年大阪府生まれ / 大阪在住 /
Masa Mode Academy of Art 研究科卒

Michinori Naro
奈路 道程

Media : Acrylic /
Pencil (DERMATOGRAPH : BLACK) / Collage
画材：アクリル絵具（ターナー）/
ペンシル（DERMATOGRAPH：BLACK）/ コラージュ

I think that I want to draw works that don't follow fashion, made with a single stroke of the hand as I cherish the feeling that what I think is good.

自分がいいと思う感じを大切にし、流行にとらわれない作品を手描き一筋で描いていきたいと思っています。

1964年高知県生まれ / 大阪在住 / 別府大学美学美術史学科卒

See more artwork（バリエーションはこちら）>> http://www.pict-web.com/michinori_naro

NICO
NICO

Media : Illustrator 10.0 / Photoshop 7.0
画材 : Illustrator 10.0 / Photoshop 7.0

Food packaging, fashion advertising, animation, etc. Also from now, I think I'd like to try to make individual characters, and have them be active in various fields.

食品のパッケージ、ファッション広告、アニメーションなど。また今後、個性的なキャラクターを作って様々な分野で活躍させてみたいと思っています。

1976年兵庫県生まれ / 大阪在住 / 嵯峨美術短期大学美術学科卒

See more artwork (バリエーションはこちら) >> http://www.pict-web.com/nico

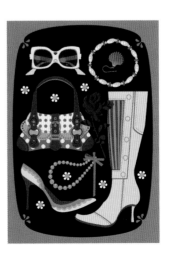

207

Izumi Nogawa
野川 いづみ

Media : Illustrator CS3 / Photoshop CS3
画材 : Illustrator CS3 / Photoshop CS3

Advertisements that feel like they have an aroma like perfume, cosmetics, etc. Packages, bottle design. Clothes, fashion accessories, decorative design for furniture. Murals on walls and ceilings. Body painting.

香水や化粧品など良い香りがしそうな広告。パッケージ、ボトルデザイン。洋服や服飾雑貨や家具の装飾用図案。壁画や天井画。ボディペイント。

東京都在住 / 女子美術大学芸術学部デザイン科環境計画卒

See more artwork（バリエーションはこちら）>> http://www.pict-web.com/izumi_nogawa

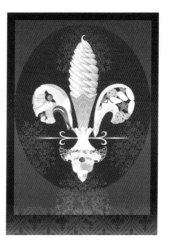

IDEAL APPARTMENT HOUSE

Muffin

DOUGHNUT

CUPCAKE

CANDL

ICE CREAM

CHOCOLATE

SCONE

Makiko Noda
ノダマキコ

My aim is to add "zest" by drawing with the sense I cut out of the everyday. I'll be happy if I can do work that has room to imagine, and excites people who see it. I want to challenge myself in various things, fashion illustration, book design.

日常を切り取る感覚で、そこに「面白み」を描き足すことが目標です。想像する余地のある、面白いと気になってもらえるような仕事が出来れば嬉しいです。ファッションイラスト、本の装丁、色々挑戦したいです。

Media : Acrylic gouache / Pencil / Color pencil / Collage
画材：ガッシュ / 鉛筆 / 色鉛筆 / コラージュ

1981年神戸生まれ / 神戸在住 / 成安造形短期大学デザイン専攻科卒

PERMANENT CAFE
PERMANENT CAFE

Children's toys, fashion.

子どものおもちゃ、ファッション。

Media : Acrylic
画材：アクリル

1971年神奈川県生まれ / 千葉県在住 /
バンタンデザイン研究所ヴィジュアル科卒

Hitomi Hasegawa
長谷川 ひとみ

Media : Color ink / Water color
画材：カラーインク / 透明水彩

1976年新潟県生まれ / 東京在住 / 長岡造形大学視覚デザイン科卒

Large dimensions like shop murals, billboards, etc. I'd also like to try my hand at work having to do with apparel like t-shirts, bags, etc.

店舗の壁面やビルボードなど面積の大きいもの。Tシャツやバッグなど、アパレル関係のお仕事も手掛けてみたいです。

See more artwork（バリエーションはこちら）>> http://www.pict-web.com/hitomi_hasegawa

は

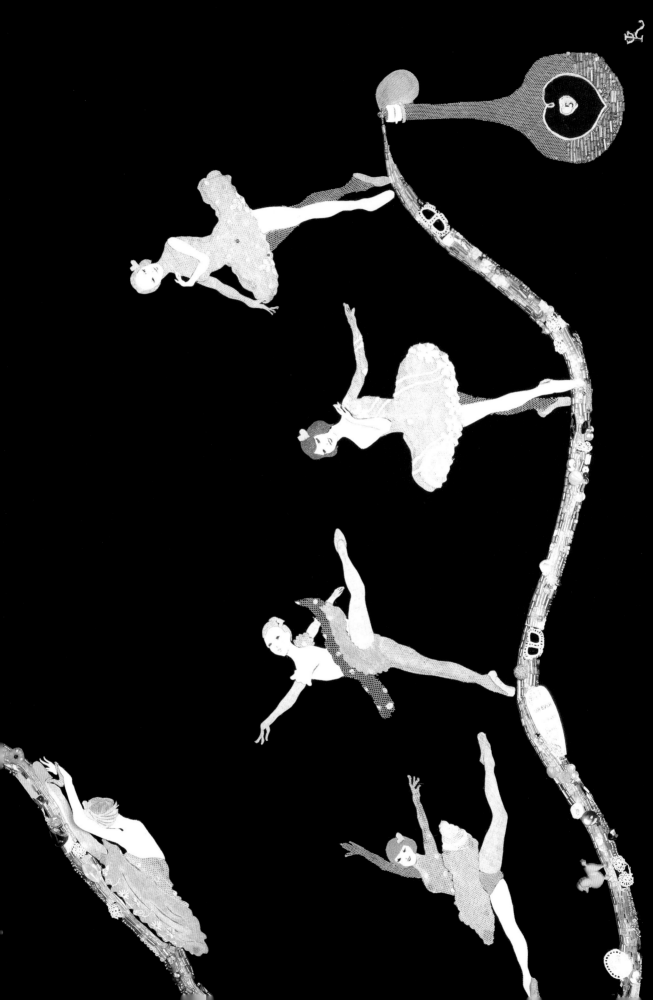

Yoko Hasegawa
長谷川 洋子

Media : Antique lace / Bead / Kimono cloth /
Accessories / Old metro ticket / Shell / Old stamp
画材：アンティークレース / ビーズ / 着物生地 / 服飾パーツ
/ 古メトロ切符 / 貝 / ヴィンテージ切手など

I've been trying to make graceful, top class works,
so I would be happy if I can do work on window
displays or collaborate with designer brands and
department stores.

高級感、気品のある作品つくりを心がけているので、百貨店や
デザイナーズブランドとのコラボレーション、ウィンドウディスプ
レイのお仕事が出来たら嬉しいです。

1981年生まれ / 多摩美術大学情報デザイン学科卒

See more artwork (バリエーションはこちら) >> http://www.pict-web.com/yoko_hasegawa

Atsushi Hara
ハラ アツシ

Media : Photoshop CS2 / Gouache / Pencil
画材：Photoshop CS2 / ガッシュ / 鉛筆

I think I'd like to try my hand at things which have forms that last a long time; calendars, mugs, etc., things that tell a story; picture books, etc.

カレンダー、マグカップなどのグッズといった長く形に残るものや、絵本などの物語性のあるものを手がけてみたいと思っています。

1970年東京生まれ / 東京在住 / セツ・モードセミナー卒

See more artwork（バリエーションはこちら）>> http://www.pict-web.com/atsushi_hara

Hayato Higasa
日笠 隼人

Media : Acrylic / Color pencil
画材：アクリル / 色鉛筆

I want to empathize with artist's images that have different methods of expression, like movies advertisement, fashion magazine, CD jackets, etc, and express them.

映画広告、ファッション雑誌、CDジャケットなど、表現方法の違うアーティストのイメージを共感して表現してみたい。

1980年宮崎県生まれ / 神奈川在住 / セツ・モードセミナー卒

See more artwork（バリエーションはこちら）>> http://www.pict-web.com/hayato_higasa

は

Chinatsu Higashi
東 ちなつ

Media : Acrylic gouache / Pencil / Antiques
画材：アクリルガッシュ / 鉛筆 / アンティークパーツ

1979年生まれ / 東京都在住 / 日本大学芸術学部デザイン学科卒

I want to do feminine movie work. I'd like to create products with my own style; both work for mass media that is printed out in large volumes, and original works that people feel like they want to hang up in their room.

ガーリーな映画の仕事をしてみたい。大量印刷されるマスメディアでの仕事と部屋に飾りたくなるような1点物の作品と両方を自分らしく創りだしていきたい。

See more artwork（バリエーションはこちら）>> http://www.pict-web.com/chinatsu_higashi

Kozue Himi
氷見 こずえ

Media : Acrylic / Fusain / Pastel / Water color /
Pencil / Pen
画材：アクリル / 木炭 / パステル / 水彩 / 鉛筆 / ペン

1976年東京生まれ / 東京在住

I'd like to try my hand at any kind of work as long as people have high expectations of me.

私に期待してくれる仕事であれば、どんな仕事でも手掛けてみたいです。

See more artwork（バリエーションはこちら）>> http://www.pict-web.com/kozue_himi

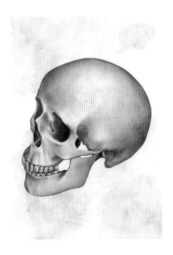

225

Tomoko Hirasawa
平澤 朋子

Media : Chinese ink / Acrylic gouache
画材：墨汁 / アクリルガッシュ

1982年東京生まれ / 東京在住 /
武蔵野美術大学視覚伝達デザイン学科卒

Book illustration, or animation. Then I would like to
do interesting work that ties my illustrations in with
making children's games or playgrounds.

書籍の挿し絵やアニメーション。そして子供の遊びや遊び場作
りにイラストレーションを関連させておもしろい事をしていきたい
です。

は

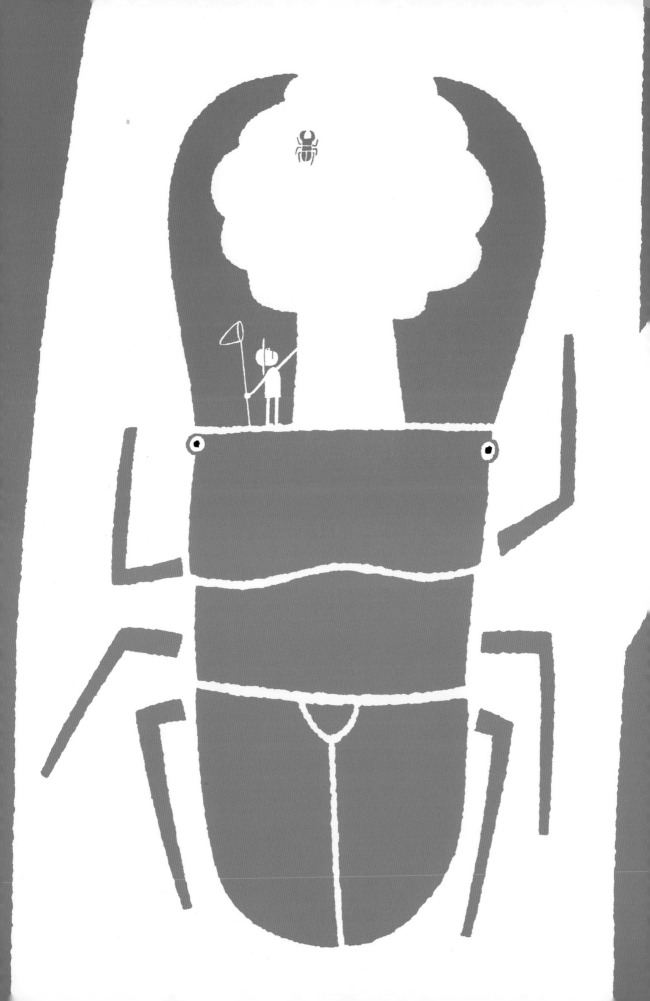

Toshiyuki Hirata
平田 利之

Media : Illustrator CS / Acrylic gouache
画材 : Illustrator CS / アクリルガッシュ

With regard to themes (from economic and politics, to amusement), I'm always dedicated to injecting ideas that have humorous twists, and expressing simple shapes and colors.

テーマ（政治経済から生活娯楽まで）に対して、ユーモアのある ひねりのきいたアイデアを盛り込み、シンプルな色と形で表現 することを常に心がけています。

1967年東京生まれ / 東京在住 /
武蔵野美術大学短期大学部デザイン科卒

は

Toshiyuki Hirano
ヒラノトシユキ

Media : Acrylic gouache / Pastel
画材 : アクリルガッシュ / パステル

I want to challenge myself in various things, book design, illustration, CD jackets, advertising, etc. I'm good at a world with a relaxing, flowing breeze.

装丁、挿絵、CDジャケット、広告など様々なものに挑戦していきたい。のんびりした空気の流れる世界が得意。

1984年生まれ / 広島出身 / 大阪在住 /
大阪デザイナー専門学校イラストレーション研究科卒

See more artwork (バリエーションはこちら) >> http://www.pict-web.com/toshiyuki_hirano

Sayaka Hirota
廣田 明香

Media : Ink / Acrylic / Waterproof pen /
Photoshop 6.0
画材 : 黒インク / アクリル / 耐水性ペン /
Photoshop 6.0

I'd like to try to work with the techniques of artisans who have inherited aspects of Japanese culture like kimono and traditional handicrafts.

着物や伝統工芸などの日本文化を引き継ぐ職人さんの技術
と、コラボレーションをしてみたいです。

1975年京都生まれ / 東京在住 / 京都精華大学デザイン学科卒

See more artwork(バリエーションはこちら) >> http://www.pict-web.com/sayaka_hirota

は

233

hiromichiito
ヒロミチイト

Media : Oil color
画材：油彩

I'm interested in work related to music.

音楽関係の仕事に興味があります。

1971年三重県生まれ / 東京都在住 /
Academy of Art University 大学院イラストレーション学科卒
(San Francisco,CA USA)

は

fantasista utamaro
ファンタジスタ歌磨呂

Media : Photoshop CS / Ink
画材：Photoshop CS / インク

I'd like to try to work with the techniques of artisans who have inherited aspects of Japanese culture like kimono and traditional handicrafts.

マンガの発想を軸に、主に海外でのプロジェクトに携わりイラストレーション、映像（アニメーション）などの活動を積極的に取り組んでいきたいです。

1979年生まれ / 東京都在住 / 多摩美術大学美術学部卒

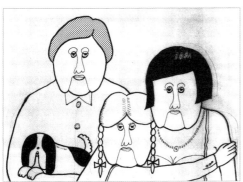

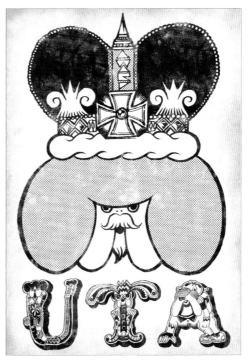

Toru Fukuda
福田 透

Media : Photoshop CS3 / Illustrator CS3 /
Painter X
画材 : Photoshop CS3 / Illustrator CS3 / Painter X

General visuals; TV shows title design, characters,
opening movie, etc., and television commercial
film's character design.

TV番組のタイトルデザインやキャラクター、オープニングムービーなどのビジュアル全般とTVCFのキャラクターデザイン。

1967年神戸生まれ / 東京在住 / 兵庫工業高校デザイン科卒

See more artwork（バリエーションはこちら）>>http://www.pict-web.com/toru_fukuda

は

HogaLee
ホガリー

Media : Ink pen / Photoshop
画材：インクペン / Photoshop

I want to try to express new forms by collaborating with other kinds of enterprises in a wide range of fields.

幅広い分野、他業種などとのコラボレーションで新しいカタチの表現をしてみたい。

1975年神奈川県生まれ / 東京在住 /
東京藝術大学デザイン科修士課程卒

は

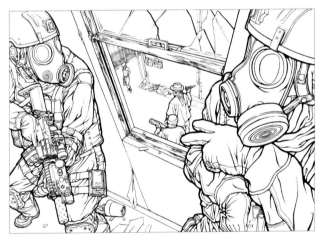

Katsuyuki Hoshino
星野 勝之

Media : Shade / Photoshop / Acrylic etc.
画材 : Shade / Photoshop / アクリル絵の具 他

I'm working mainly in editorial work like cover art, illustration, etc., but I think that if I'm able, I'd like to do concept design of actual objects, sets, etc.

装画、挿絵などエディトリアルの仕事が中心ですが現実の物体、セットなどのコンセプトデザインが出来れば、と思っています。

1976年東京都生まれ / 埼玉在住 / 日本デザイン専門学校卒

See more artwork（バリエーションはこちら）>> http://www.pict-web.com/katsuyuki_hoshino

は

243

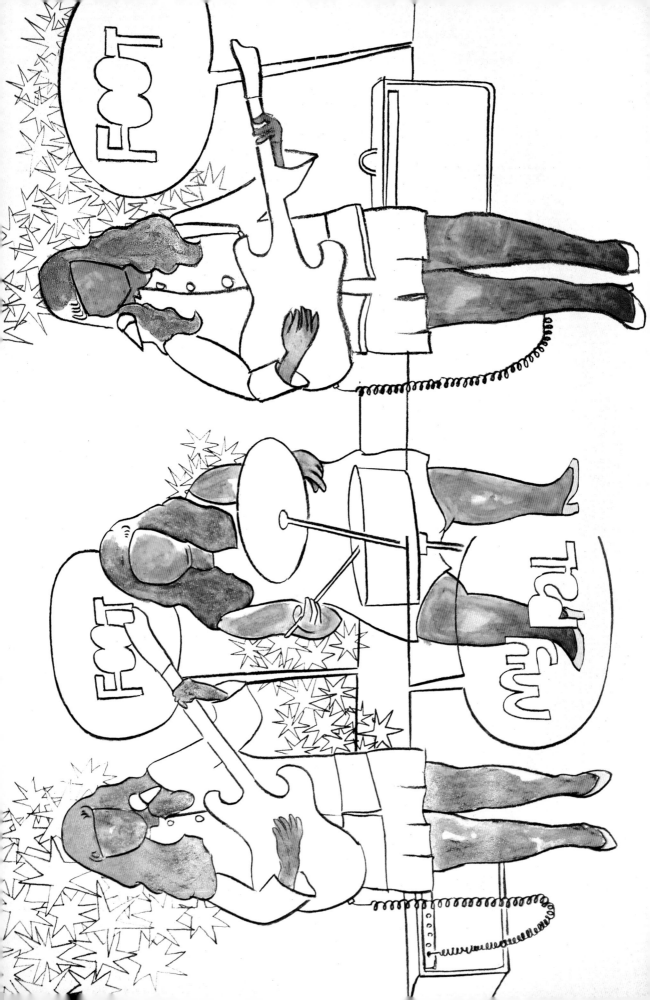

magma giants
マグマジャイアンツ

From now I'd like to try to do moving images. My dream work is the videos, etc. of the band Red Crayola.

今後は動画などやってみたいです。レッド・クレイオラのビデオとか!!!夢です。

Media : Pencil / Crayon / Acrylic / Collage
画材：鉛筆 / クレヨン / アクリル / コラージュ

1969年岩手県生まれ / 東京在住 / 桑沢デザイン研究所卒

See more artwork（バリエーションはこちら）>> http://www.pict-web.com/magma_giants

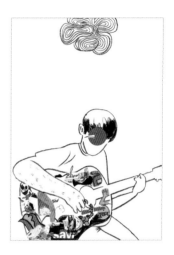

ま

MACHIKO
MACHIKO

Media : Illustrator 10.0 / Photoshop 7.0 /
Old paper / Fabric
画材 : Illustrator 10.0 / Photoshop 7.0 / 古紙 / 布

I'd like to do work in brand advertising and fashion. I'd like to apply my illustrations to not only Japanese, but also foreign brands.

ファッション、ブランド広告を手がけていきたいです。日本だけではなく海外のブランドツールとしても私のイラストを活かしていきたいです。

1983年神奈川生まれ / 兵庫在住 / デザイン事務所を経てフリーに

See more artwork (バリエーションはこちら) >> http://www.pict-web.com/machiko

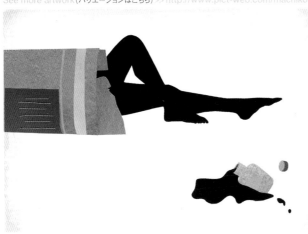

Miyuki Matsuo
松尾 ミユキ

I would like to work on things that have a bit of taste like folklore and bring out a nostalgic feeling, or book design with single color ink line drawing, literary arts magazines, cook books.

懐かしい感じのする、少しフォークロアっぽいテイスト、はたまた墨一色の線画で本の装丁や、文芸誌、料理の本の仕事をしていきたいです。

Media : Acrylic / Ink / Wax pastel
画材：アクリル / インク / ワックスパステル

1973年名古屋生まれ / 東京在住 / パレットクラブ京都校卒

See more artwork(バリエーションはこちら) >> http://www.pict-web.com/miyuki_matsuo

Kaori Matsukura
松倉 香子

Media : Water color / Photoshop CS
画材：水彩 / アクリル / Photoshop CS

1969年東京生まれ / 東京在住 / 専修大学文学部国文学科卒

I don't want to be limited by specific work, I want to challenge myself in various things, I want to make the kind of things I've never seen before.

この仕事という限定をせずに、いろいろなことにチャレンジし、今までみたことがないようなモノを作っていきたい。

Satoshi Matsuzawa
マツザワ サトシ

Media : Mechanical pensil / Illustrator 8.0 /
Photoshop 4.0
画材：シャープペンシル / Illustrator 8.0 /
Photoshop 4.0

Until now, I've mostly been doing digital production of illustrations, however, I'd also like to branch
into producing analog works (acrylic, etc.)

今までデジタル制作のイラストがメインでしたが、アナログ制作
（アクリルなど）の作品群も創っていきたいです。

1967年大阪府生まれ / 栃木在住 / 青山学院大学卒

See more artwork（バリエーションはこちら）>> http://www.pict-web.com/satoshi_matsuzawa

mashcomix
マッシュコミックス

From now on I'd like to continue to do various creative activities, revolving around comic books, design, and art, not only in two dimensions.

今後もマンガ、デザイン、アートを軸に、平面だけに留まらず、様々な制作活動をしていきたいです。

Media : Photoshop / Illustrator / Pen / Pencil / Ink
画材 : Photoshop / Illustrator / ペン / 鉛筆 / インク

東京芸術大学卒 / 多摩美術大学美術学部卒

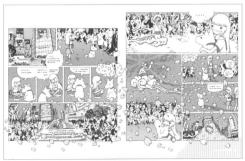

Shiho Matsubara
松原 シホ

Media : Illustrator 10.0
画材 : Illustrator 10.0

Fashion, foreign literature's cover art.

ファッション、海外文学の装画。

1971年東京生まれ / 東京在住 / 早稲田大学政治経済学部政治学科卒

See more artwork（バリエーションはこちら）>> http://www.pict-web.com/shiho_matsubara

ま

Mariko Matsumoto
松元 まり子

I'm interested in things that tell a story; picture books, picture-card shows, animation, comics, etc.

ストーリーのあるもの、絵本、紙芝居、アニメーション、漫画など興味があります。

Media : Water color / Color pencil
画材：水彩 / 色鉛筆

1967年名古屋生まれ / 名古屋在住 / セツ・モードセミナー卒

See more artwork（バリエーションはこちら）>> http://www.pict-web.com/mariko_matsumoto

ま

259

Mio Matsumoto
松本 美緒

Media : Pen / Photoshop / Illustrator /
Color pencil / Gouache / Crayon
画材：ペン / Photoshop / Illustrator / 色鉛筆 /
ガッシュ / クレヨン

I think that I'd like to do work relating to corporate identity like advertisements. Personally I'm carrying on with making books based on diaries, so I'm also interested in things related to publishing.

広告など企業のアイデンティティに関わる仕事をしてみたいと思っています。個人的には日記をベースにした本の制作を進めているので、出版関係にも興味があります。

1976年兵庫県生まれ / 東京在住 / イギリス Royal College of Art (RCA),
communication art and design科卒

micca
micca

Media : Water color / Acrylic / Pencil
画材：水彩 / アクリル / 鉛筆

I want to do things like movies, theater posters, or pamphlets. I really love books, so from now I think it would be good if I can be involved in lots of books. Also, I would like to increase activity in other countries, so that I can meet different kinds of people through pictures.

映画や演劇のポスターやパンフレットなどやってみたいです。本がとても好きなのでこれからも多くの本に関わっていけたらと思っています。また海外での活動を増やして絵を通じていろんな人と出会っていきたいです。

三重県生まれ / 東京在住 / 京都精華大学美術学部洋画専攻卒

See more artwork（バリエーションはこちら）>> http://www.pict-web.com/micca

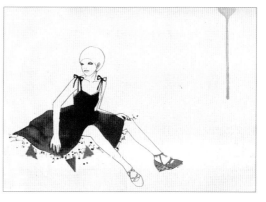

ま

MICAO
ミカオ

Media : Cloth / Embroidery thread /
Paint for fablics
画材：布 / 刺しゅう糸 / 布用絵の具

Book cover art, illustration, CD jacket, picture
books etc. I want to draw illustrations that remain
widely in people's hearts and, through warmth and
humor, make use of the feeling of the material in
embroidery.

本の装画、挿絵、CDのジャケット、絵本など。刺繍の素材感
を生かした、暖かで、ユーモラスな、そして、広く心に残るイラス
トを描きたいです。

1967年生まれ / 神戸市在住 / ギャラリーvie絵話塾卒

See more artwork（バリエーションはこちら）>> http://www.pict-web.com/micao

Satomi Mizuuchi
みずうち さとみ

Media : Gauze / Embroidery thread /
Paints for fablics
画材：ガーゼ / 刺しゅう糸 / 布描き絵具

I want to challenge myself in various things like book design, picture books, animation, etc. I want to live everyday pleasantly as I draw funny and interesting pictures.

装丁、絵本、アニメーションなど、いろいろなものにチャレンジしたいです。おもしろおかしい絵を描いて、毎日愉快に暮らしたいです。

1972年埼玉生まれ / 東京在住 / セツ・モードセミナー卒

See more artwork（バリエーションはこちら）>> http://www.pict-web.com/satomi_mizuuchi

Atsushi Mizukami
ミズカミ アツシ

Media : Illustrator CS3 / Photoshop CS3
画材 : Illustrator CS3 / Photoshop CS3

Book design / illustrations, cover art and illustration for novels (mysteries, light novels, etc.), electronic music related artwork, animation, and comic books.

書籍の装丁画、小説(ミステリ物やライトノベルなど)の表紙絵や挿絵、電子音楽系のアートワーク、アニメーション、漫画。

1976年山形県生まれ / 東京在住 / 仙台デザイン専門学校卒

Kenichiro Mizuno
水野 健一郎

Media : Pencil / Photoshop 7.0
画材：鉛筆 / Photoshop 7.0

CD jackets, book design, advertising, music videos, and original animation. And also, I would like to challenge myself in a wide variety of work without being choosy about genres.

CDジャケット、装丁、広告、ミュージックビデオ、オリジナルアニメーション。その他ジャンルにこだわらず様々な仕事に挑戦したいです。

1967年岐阜県生まれ / 東京在住 / セツ・モードセミナー卒

See more artwork（バリエーションはこちら）>> http://www.pict-web.com/kenichiro_mizuno

ま

Aki Miyajima
宮島 亜希

Media : Ballpoint pen / Pencil / Pigment / Chinese ink / Photoshop 5.5
画材 : 水性ボールペン / 鉛筆 / 顔彩 / 墨汁 / Photoshop 5.5

I want to be broadly active in print media like fashion magazines, signs, the web, etc. However, I want to, without pushing myself, provide works that attract the people who see them.

ファッション誌などの紙媒体、またサインやwebなど、幅広く活動したいですが、自分に無理をせず見る人を惹き付けられる作品を提供してきたいです。

1979年滋賀県生まれ / 東京在住 / 京都芸術デザイン専門学校デザイン総合学科卒

See more artwork (バリエーションはこちら) >> http://www.pict-web.com/aki_miyajima

ま

Jiro Miyata
ミヤタ ジロウ

Media : Illustrator CS3 / Photoshop CS3
画材 : Illustrator CS3 / Photoshop CS3

I think that it would be great if I can do the kind of work that makes use of the comfort that scenes have.

風景が持つ心地よさを生かせるような仕事ができればいいなと思います。

1972年大阪府生まれ / 大阪府在住

See more artwork（バリエーションはこちら）>> http://www.pict-web.com/jiro_miyata

Ryoko Mutoh
武藤 良子

Media : Oil pastel
画材：オイルパステル

Paper-print works like book design, illustration, movies, theater posters, etc. Textile design like fabrics. I would like to try to do anything that makes use of my pictures.

書籍の装丁、挿画、映画、演劇のポスターなどの紙もの。布地などのテキスタイルデザイン。絵を活かせるものならなんでも試してみたいです。

1971年東京生まれ / 東京在住 / セツ・モードセミナー卒

277

mogu
mogu

Media : Socks / Gloves / Used clothes /
Acrylic gouache / Fimo / Corrugated board etc.
画材：くつした / てぶくろ / 古着 / アクリルガッシュ /
フィモ / ダンボールなど

Recently I have been mainly involved in exhibitions, so I'm interested in magazines, advertisements, web, etc. regardless of the genre.

現在は主に、展覧会を中心とした活動をおこなっているので、雑誌や広告、ウェブなど、ジャンルをとわず興味をもっております。

1984年東京生まれ

mocchi mocchi
mocchi mocchi

Media : Silk screen
画材：シルクスクリーン

I want to feel the charm of products that have warmth and texture; natural cloth fabric, traditional dyeing techniques, etc. I want to try my hand at design that takes advantage of the feeling of those kind of materials within the field of interior design.

自然素材の布や伝統的な染色法など、暖かさや風合いをもつ商品に魅力を感じます。インテリアの分野でそういった素材感を活かしたデザインを手がけたい。

望月佐知子(姉)・純子(妹) / 共に大阪在住、Masa Mode Academy卒

See more artwork（バリエーションはこちら）>> http://www.pict-web.com/mocchi_mocchi

Toru Morooka
師岡 とおる
(more rock art all)

Media : Fabric / Felt / String / Linestone /
Wappen / Silk screen
画材：布 / フエルト / 糸 / 綿 / ラインストーン /
ワッペン / シルクスクリーン

1972年東京生まれ / 東京在住 /
武蔵野美術大学空間演出デザイン学科卒

Work in which I can try new things.

新しいことを試せる仕事。

See more artwork（バリエーションはこちら）>> http://www.pict-web.com/toru_morooka

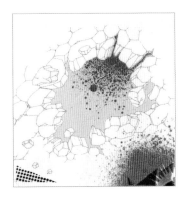

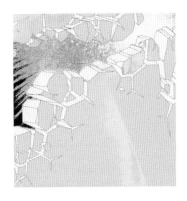

Emi Yamaguchi
山口 絵美

Media : Illustrator CS
画材 : Illustrator CS

1971年東京都生まれ / 東京都在住 /
青山学院女子短期大学芸術学科卒

First of all, I would like to express faithfully what I want to say to the people who see them. And furthermore I think it would be better if I could add some extra taste of fun and enjoyment.

見る人に伝えたいことを、まずはきちんと表現できたらよいと思います。さらにプラスアルファの楽しみやおかしみが加えられたら尚よいと思います。

See more artwork (バリエーションはこちら) >> http://www.pict-web.com/emi_yamaguchi

Mariko Yamazaki
山崎 真理子

I think I want to move toward doing work that isn't bound by genre. From now, the areas I would like to expand into are books, novel illustration, and fashion.

ジャンルにとらわれることなく仕事をしていきたいと思っています。今後広げていきたい分野は、書籍や小説の挿絵、ファッション関係のイラストなど。

Media : Illustrator 8.0 / Photoshop CS3
画材 : Illustrator 8.0 / Photoshop CS3

1975年大阪生まれ / 大阪在住 /
大阪デザイナー専門学校グラフィックデザイン科卒

See more artwork（バリエーションはこちら）>> http://www.pict-web.com/mariko_yamazaki

287

Ryohei Yamashita
山下 良平

Media : Photoshop CS / Painter 9 / Acrylic
画材 : Photoshop CS / Painter 9 / アクリル

I want to do work in which when people think of drawings with "YAKUDOO" (means dynamic action in Japanese), they think of Yamashita.

「躍動」する絵といえば山下と言われるような仕事をしたい。

1973年福岡生まれ / 横浜市在住 / 九州芸術工科大学卒

や

NOBUO YAMADA
山田 ノブオ

I'm happy if I can continue the kind of picture work that can live in any time period or anywhere, that doesn't just follow fashion.

単に流行に左右されないような、どの時代でもどこかで生きているような絵仕事を続けていけたらシアワセです。

Media : Flash 4 / Illustrator 8.0 / Photoshop 6.0
画材 : Flash 4 / Illustrator 8.0 / Photoshop 6.0

1962年東京生まれ / 東京在住 / 阿佐ヶ谷美術専門学校卒

See more artwork（バリエーションはこちら）>> http://www.pict-web.com/nobuo_yamada

や

icebox drea

free
time

Mamoru Yamamoto
山本 まもる

Media : Photoshop CS / Carbon paper /
Ballpoint pen / Copy paper
画材：Photoshop CS / カーボン紙 / ボールペン /
コピー用紙

Work like animation and characters that seem to
walk by themselves.

アニメーションやキャラが1人歩きしそうなお仕事。

1960年東京生まれ / 横浜在住 / 桑沢デザイン研究所卒

や

stav Cramer plays with pictorial truth but by recreating it. The guise through which his emo d journeys are revealed – recently, photographic represe andscape – grants us a false sense of security towards the subje c gradually evaporates under the weight of our gaze. Cramer's tril ries that began in 2002 – 'Woodland', 'Underwater', 'Mountain' – w ts painterly frame of reference (and perhaps the artist's German her itage) has prompted alignment of his practice with Neo-Romantic pho

or combinatio
ped from the unkno
and inherited moments
of time, et the thoughts the
rial and had to grasp, snaggin
like fabric pul ed through the tee

SUNDAY

RIAN HORWATH

isplay

BRUXELLES

Yuko Yamamoto
山本 祐布子

Media : Paper
画材 : 紙

I think from now on, I want to further increase works which I make for someone else, like works in which I make as I'm calling to mind another person's face, like works I make together with someone else in a united effort.

相手がいて、その人の顔を思い浮かべながら作るもの、誰かと一緒に力を合わせて作るもの、そういう、誰かのためのもの作りを、今後はもっと増やしていきたいと思います。

1977年東京生まれ / 東京在住 / 京都精華大学デザイン学科卒

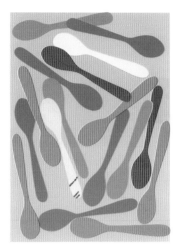

Yukarina
YUKARINA

Media : Color pencil / Acrylic
画材：色鉛筆 / アクリル

I specialize in drawing motifs of animals, nature etc., like trees and birds, so I want to try to do work in which those kind of things are necessary. Also, cover art that demands abstract emotional expression.

木や鳥など自然や動物などのモチーフを描くのが得意なのでそういったものが必要とされる仕事をしてみたい。また抽象的な感情表現を求められる装画です。

1979年香川県生まれ / 香川在住 / 京都インターナショナルアカデミー卒

Kaori Yoshioka
吉岡 香織

Media : Photoshop CS2
画材 : Photoshop CS2

I want to be involved in work related to fashion.
Animation.

モードに関する仕事に携わりたい。アニメーション。

1974年広島生まれ / 東京在住 / 文化服装学院卒

See more artwork (バリエーションはこちら) >> http://www.pict-web.com/kaori_yoshioka

や

Yuko Yoshioka
吉岡 ゆうこ

Media : Photoshop 7.0 / Pencil / Acrylic
画材 : Photoshop 7.0 / 鉛筆 / アクリル 他

Images, moving pictures such as music videos or TV commercial messages. And I really like movies, so I'd like to draw advertisements having to do with movies.

ミュージックビデオやTVCMなどの映像、動画。それと映画が大好きなので映画関連の広告などを描いてみたいです。

1972年東京生まれ / 東京在住 /
武蔵野美術短期大学空間演出デザインコース卒

See more artwork（バリエーションはこちら）>> http://www.pict-web.com/yuko_yoshioka

や

Megumi Yoshizane
吉實 恵

Media : Liquitex / Water color / Oil paints
画材：リキテックス / 水彩絵の具 / 油絵の具

I want to do both works; one is slowly communicated with people like picture books; the other is what represents their era like movies, fashion, etc. I'm interested in people, so I want to draw portraits.

モード、映画などその時代を表すもの、絵本のようにゆっくり伝えていくもの、両方やっていきたい。人間に興味があるので、ポートレートを描きたいです。

1970年千葉生まれ / 東京在住 / 武蔵野美術大学卒

See more artwork（バリエーションはこちら）>> http://www.pict-web.com/megumi_yoshizane

や

303

Hisanori Yoshida
吉田 尚令

Media : Color ink / Acrylic gouache
画材：カラーインク / アクリルガッシュ

1971年大阪生まれ / 大阪在住 / 京都インターナショナルアカデミー卒

I want to make picture books. I want to create not only pictures, but also my own stories. I want to work without constraints. I want to draw better pictures.

絵本を創りたいです。絵はもちろん、お話も自分自身で創作したい。仕事はこだわりなく何だってしたい。より良い絵を描きたい。

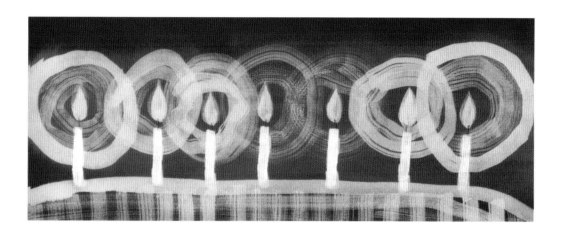

Asako Yoshihama
吉濱 あさこ

Media : Photoshop CS3 / Acrylic
画材 : Photoshop CS3 / アクリル絵の具

I think that I want to do work related to apparel,
like fashion advertising, goods, etc.

ファッション関係の広告や、グッズなど、アパレルに関するお仕
事をしたいと思っています。

東京在住 / 沖縄県立芸術大学デザイン学科卒

See more artwork (バリエーションはこちら) >> http://www.pict-web.com/asako_yoshihama

や

Licaco
Licaco

Media : Photoshop CS3
画材 : Photoshop CS3

Any work related to fashion. Also, packaging, CD jackets, novel covers, etc. I want to challenge myself in my interest in moving images.

ファッション関係のお仕事はなんでも。あと、パッケージやCDジャケット、小説のカバーなど。動画にも興味があり、挑戦していきたいです。

神戸生まれ / 東京在住

See more artwork(バリエーションはこちら) >> http://www.pict-web.com/licaco

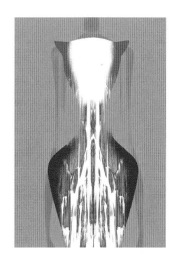

room-composite
room-composite

room-composite

I aim for pictures that create a balance between design and illustration; pictures that draw by intuition, not by figures, not decor, nor explanations, pictures that make air that can't be verbalized.

デザインとイラストレーションの均衡を行き交う画。図では無く地で描く画。装飾でも説明でも無く、言語化できない空気を作る画。を目指しています。

Media : Photoshop CS3 / Illustrator CS3
画材 : Photoshop CS3 / Illustrator CS3

1975年兵庫県生まれ / 東京在住 / 大阪デザイナー専門学校卒

See more artwork (バリエーションはこちら) >> http://www.pict-web.com/room_composite

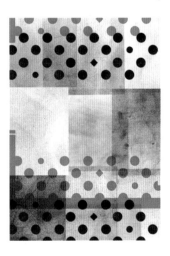

ら

Illustrator index (Alphabetical order)

Illustrator index イラストレーター・インデックス

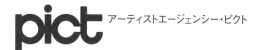 アーティストエージェンシー・ピクト

3つのメディアがつながるピクト。

iLLUSTRATiON BOOK PRO 01·02

日本発、世界をリードするイラスト
レーターをコンセプトにピクトが
セレクトした150名の描き下ろし
作品を収録。ピエ・ブックスより国内、
海外の書店にて発売中。

出版

pictでは

出版、ギャラリー、ウェブの3つのメディアを
連動させ、日本のイラストレーターを国内のみ
ならず、海外へ向けて発信しています。

pict
ピクト

ギャラリー ━━━━ ウェブ

pict:gallery

イラスト、写真、映像などジャンルにとらわれず、今、
そしてこれからを担うクリエイティブを発信するレン
タルギャラリー。www.pict-web.com/pg

pict:web

ピクトに登録する全250名のイラストレーターの
新作、仕事実績などの他、作品展情報やインタビュー
などの最新情報を掲載。www.pict-web.com

250名を超えるイラストレーターが登録する pict

ピクトではイラストのオリジナル制作をコーディネートから進行管理、納品までトータルにバックアップ。レンタル可能な
作品も豊富に取り揃えています。経験豊かなエージェントスタッフがお客様のご要望を的確に捉え、訴求力ある質の
高いクリエイティブに貢献します。また、ロンドンのアーティストエージェンシーDutchUncleとの提携により、海外との
ネットワークも活かしたインターナショナルなコーディネートも行っています。ピクトは日本を代表するアーティスト
エージェンシーです。

イラストなら差がつく<ruby>差<rt>サガツク</rt></ruby>ピクトへ。

イラストレーターが決まっていない時・・・

最適なイラストレーターをセレクト

国内、海外に広くコネクションをもつピクトのコーディネーターが、プロジェクトに応じたイラストレーターのピックアップ、デザインカンプに使えるデータの手配を承ります。

サガピク

例えば・・
大学生をターゲットにした年間プロモーションに提案出来るイラストレーターを探して欲しい。

コーディネート例

イラストレーターが決まっている時・・・

イラストのオリジナル制作をサポート

豊富な実績をもつピクトのエージェントスタッフが、イラストのオリジナル制作において、予算、スケジュールの管理、ご要望に確実に応えられるようイラストディレクション、マネジメントを行います。

ツクピク

例えば・・
イラストレーターの○○さんにファッションビルのポスター用イラスト1点を描いて欲しい。

オリジナル制作例

サガツクブラザー

探してピクト、創ってピクトに関するお問い合わせは下記までお願い致します。

info@pict-web.com

ピクトはアスタリスク、ヴィジョントラックにより運営されています。

（東日本エリア）（有）アスタリスク ＊asterisk

TEL **03-5766-4625**
107-0062 東京都港区南青山5-10-14
オークリッジ南青山201

（西日本エリア）（有）ヴィジョントラック vision track

TEL **06-6316-7363**
530-0047 大阪市北区西天満2-8-1大江ビル210

PICT-WEB.COM

イラストのオリジナル制作&レンタルはピクト、
登録イラストレーター約250名の最新情報はここでチェック！

Top

日本を代表するイラストレーターが集結

PICT-WEB.COMには日本を代表するアーティストエージェンシー・ピクトが厳選したイラストレーターのみが掲載されていますので、ここをチェックすればイラストレーションの動向が分かります。

A page of illustrator

プレゼンに必要な情報は全てここに

登録イラストレーターの最新作、仕事実績、詳細プロフィールなど、プレゼンに必要な情報が全て用意されています。

Stock illustration

レンタル可能なストックイラスト

掲載イラストレーター全員のストックイラストも多数用意、次々と新作がアップされています。限られた時間での高い要求にも応えられる、妥協無いクリエイティブを提供します。

イラストなら差がつくピクトのサービス！

最適なイラストレーターをコーディネートする「探してピクト」、イラストのオリジナル制作をフルにサポートする「創ってピクト」もPICT-WEB.COMよりお問い合わせ、ご依頼いただけます。

イラストのオリジナル制作&レンタルはピクト

≫ www.pict-web.com

無料のメンバー登録でプレゼンに使えるカンプデータがダウンロードできます！

PICT GALLERY

ピクトがプロデュースするレンタルギャラリー。
今、そして、これからを担うアートを世界へ。

プロ仕様なアートギャラリー

アーティストエージェンシーとしての国内、海外への幅広い
ネットワークを活かしながら、アーティストを積極的にサポー
トし、イラストレーションを軸に、ヴィジュアルコンテンツとし
て成立するものであれば、写真、映像、立体作品なども取り
上げ、これからを担うクリエイティブを発信していきます。

歴史的な建築物「大江ビルヂング」

大正モダンと和が融合されたデザインで多くの人を魅了し
続けている大江ビルヂング内にあるpict:gallery。あらゆる
ジャンルのアートが映える魅力ある空間です。

アーティストの作品ファイル

pict:gallery、2Fにミニギャラリースペースとアーティストの
作品ファイルが閲覧できるスペース「pict:salon」がオー
プンしました。ギャラリー展示アーティスト、そしてpict登録
アーティストの最新作や仕事実績がご覧頂けます。プレゼン
などでイラスト等をお探しの方には最高の資料室となって
おりますので是非お越しください。

pict:gallery

530-0047 大阪市北区西天満2-8-1大江ビル110
TEL 06-6316-7363 FAX 06-6316-7365
（TELはvision trackがお受け致します。）

mail:pg@pict-web.com

＊ギャラリーレンタルのお問い合わせお申し込みは上記までお願いします。

Illustration Book Pro 02

イラストレーション ブック プロ 02

2008年10月1日　初版第1刷発行

企画・制作・編集：有限会社アスタリスク　有限会社ヴィジョントラック

ジャケットデザイン：atmosphere ltd.（川村 哲司）

デザイン：イマイ ヤスフミ

DTP：柴 亜季子

制作進行：関本 康弘

発行者：三芳 伸吾

発行所：ピエ・ブックス　〒170-0005 東京都豊島区南大塚2-32-4

編集　TEL：03-5395-4820　FAX：03-5395-4821　e-mail：editor@piebooks.com
営業　TEL：03-5395-4811　FAX：03-5395-4812　e-mail：sales@piebooks.com
http://www.piebooks.com

印刷：図書印刷株式会社

Printed in Japan

ISBN978-4-89444-722-6 C3070

©2008 asterisk / vision track / PIE BOOKS

本書の収録内容の無断転載、複写、引用等を禁じます。落丁・乱丁はお取り替え致します。

掲載作品のご使用に関する問い合わせは下記までお願い致します。

有限会社アスタリスク　　〒107-0062 東京都港区南青山5-10-14　TEL：03-5766-4625　FAX：03-5766-4743
有限会社ヴィジョントラック 〒530-0047 大阪府北区西天満2-8-1　大江ビル210　TEL：06-6316-7363　FAX：06-6316-7365

http://www.pict-web.com
e-mail：info@pict-web.com

Illustration Book Pro 02

Date of Publication：1st October 2008

Planning and Production : asterisk inc. vision track inc.

Jacket Design : atmosphere ltd.（Tetsushi Kawamura）

Design : Yasufumi Imai

DTP : Akiko Shiba

Coordinator : Yasuhiro Sekimoto

Publisher : Shingo Miyoshi

Publishing Company : PIE BOOKS　2-32-4, Minami-Otsuka, Toshima-ku, Tokyo 170-0005 JAPAN
Tel : +81-3-5395-4811　Fax : +81-3-5395-4812
http://www.piebooks.com
e-mail：editor@piebooks.com
e-mail：sales@piebooks.com

Printed in Japan

ISBN978-4-89444-722-6

©2008 asterisk / vision track / PIE BOOKS

All rights reserved. No part of this publication may be reproduced in
any form or by any means, graphic, electronic or mechanical,
including photocopying and recording by an information storage
and retrieval system, without permission in writing from the publisher.

Inquiry about contents :

asterisk inc.
5-10-14, Minami-Aoyama, Minato-ku, Tokyo 107-0062 JAPAN
Tel : +81-3-5766-4625　Fax : +81-3-5766-4743

vision track inc.
2nd Floor Oe Bldg. 2-8-1, Nishitenma, Kita-ku, Osaka 530-0047 JAPAN
Tel : +81-6-6316-7363　Fax : +81-6-6316-7365

http://www.pict-web.com
e-mail : info@pict-web.com